Tom Loud has been a personal hero and friend for many years. I have learned so much from his YouTube channel, from watching his life lived out for Jesus, and now from him as an author. I could not put this book down. Every chapter is full of incredible wisdom, encouragement, and empowerment. Tom provides crystal clarity on what Jesus has done for us and what He wants to do through us. The miracle stories will bring tears to your eyes, and the teaching will take limits off of your thinking. *Unlocking Kingdom Power* is a must-read for any believer who wants to manifest Jesus to the world!

— JASON CHIN, FOUNDER OF LOVE
SAYS GO MINISTRIES

Unlocking Kingdom Power will convince you that God's miraculous power is available to all who dare to believe. Get this book. Read it, apply it, and watch God show up!

— DAVID STEWART, FOUNDER AND
PASTOR OF ARIZONA HEALING
ROOMS

D1590510

Unlocking Kingdom Power takes all of the complexity and confusion out of an area the institutional church has struggled with for generations. This is one of those books that isn't written as theory, but as powerful truths that Tom has practiced and lived out himself. Tom's style makes these truths very accessible and easy to grasp. I am humbled and challenged by this book. I believe it is going to shatter doubts and help readers fully walk in God's truth.

> — PETE CABRERA JR, EVANGELIST
> AND DIRECTOR OF ROYAL FAMILY
> INTERNATIONAL UNIVERSITY

UNLOCKING KINGDOM POWER

Five Keys to Divine Healing

TOM LOUD

CALLED WRITERS
CHRISTIAN PUBLISHING

COPYRIGHT

Published by Called Writers Christian Publishing, LLC

Tuscaloosa, Alabama

Print version ISBN: 978-1-7354760-5-6

I would like to dedicate this book to my wife, Paula, and my mother-in-law, Maria. Thank you for your unwavering love, support, and prayers all these years as I have embarked on the journey of full-time ministry.

CONTENTS

Introduction   11

1. THE KEYS EXIST   21
Reaching the Lost with Miracles   22
Bobby   24
Jaden   29
We All Have Questions   31
God's Truth versus Personal Experience   32
Are Miracles for Me?   34
A Mangled Leg Is Restored   36

2. THE NATURE OF THE KEYS   41
Knowledge of the Keys   45
The Keys Must Be Used   47
The Spirit Realm   49
Where Are the Keys?   50

3. THE KEY OF IDENTITY   53
Called and Equipped   58
Identity Determines Rights   59
Identity Determines Authority   63
Why Our Identity Matters So Much   65
God's Word Is Trustworthy   68
The New Creation   70

4. THE KEY OF AUTHORITY   75
Believe the Word   76
You Are God's Plan A and He Has No   78
Plan B
The Throne of God   80
I Have, I Give   82
Do I Have the Gift of Healing?   86

Your Authority Is Enough   89
The Source of All Authority   91
Faith Through the Faithless   94

5. THE KEY OF OVERCOMING THE   99
   CARNAL MIND
The Day I Learned Nothing   101
The Beauty of Nothing   106
Put Your Carnal Mind in the Corner   112
Bringing Your Carnal Mind into   114
Subjection
My First Experience Thinking Nothing   118
The Carnal Mind and the Enemy   124
Embracing Christ in You   126

6. THE KEY OF WALKING IN THE   129
   SPIRIT MIND
Mind, Submit to Spirit   130
Cleaning Out the Closet   133
The Natural Mind versus the Spiritual   136
God's Promises Are Right Now   138
From the Footstool to the Throne   140
Claiming Your New Mind   141
When to Stop Praying   143
The Mind of a Zebra   144
What is Spiritual Warfare, Really?   145
Godlike Faith   149
Childlike Faith   151

7. THE KEY OF CALLING   155
You Have Been Called   155
A New Creation in Christ   157
God's Own Heart   158
What You Are Made to Do   161
The New Ways of the New Man   163
Who Am I Called to Heal?   166

8. FISHING FOR PEOPLE   169
   A Responsibility and an Honor   171
   Go Where the Fish Are   173
   Good Works in Action   175
   Finding Fish   177
   Ready, Set, Action!   180
   Physical Healing versus Pain Healing   182
   You Can Do This!   185
   Go!   187

   Acknowledgments   191
   Publisher's Note: An Invitation to   193
   Paradise
   Recent Releases from Called Writers   199
   About the Author   203

INTRODUCTION

My ministry has seen God perform thousands of healing miracles. Every time I go out to minister healing to people, I see people healed. My overall success rate runs somewhere between 70-80%, meaning that when I pray for someone to be healed, they experience some level of healing 70-80% of the time. Of course, none of this is because of anything special about me. As a believer in Jesus, you can get the same results. In this book, I'm going to teach you how to operate with that same type of success for healing miracles. But first, I'd like to give you some background on my journey.

MY FAITH JOURNEY

When I was 17 years old, my major ambition in life was to become the next Bruce Lee. Achieving the status of a well-known martial arts expert was my burning desire.

It was all I wanted, so I trained day and night to achieve this goal. Martial arts and the pursuit of fame were my great passions. But something came along and changed the course of my life completely: I met Jesus Christ.

I was not brought up in a Christian household. The only thing I knew about God was what a Catholic friend of mine had once told me. He had explained, "You cannot go to Heaven unless you are baptized." That was the extent of my theological training. But at the age of 17, everything changed.

The city I grew up in was not what you would call racially diverse. While working as a busboy at a restaurant, I met a black man for the very first time. His name was Tom, just like mine. He was from a completely different world—one I had never even heard about. I was not even aware that this world existed.

I started getting to know Tom a little, and he said that we should talk after work one day. He wanted to tell me about some bizarre supernatural things that I had never heard of before. I was curious, so I took the bait, agreeing to meet after work and talk to him.

The talk with my friend Tom was unlike anything I had ever experienced. Looking back, I realize that for the first time in my life, someone was explaining the Gospel message to me. Something inside of me—a sort of longing, a deep desire, and a thirst that was unquenchable—began to grow. I felt compelled to seek more information, so I kept asking more questions. As I listened intently, he told me of things that were otherworldly. I sat shocked, struggling to believe that I had never heard of these things before.

Tom told me about the baptism in the Holy Spirit and speaking in tongues. Then there were some other claims that stretched the bounds of credulity. Still, I wanted to hear more.

Next, he told me that if I wanted to be saved, I would need to repent of my sins and turn to Jesus. These were very foreign concepts to me, but before I knew it, these words came out of my mouth: "That's what I need. Please show me the way."

Tom invited me to come to church with him the next Sunday. As it turned out, his dad was the pastor of an all-black Pentecostal church. I said I would attend, but I wanted a favor from him, if possible. Remembering what my Catholic friend had said about the need to be baptized with water, I asked Tom if he could get his father to baptize me for free, me being Tom's co-worker and all.

Tom told me he was sure he could swing that! Next thing you know, I was the only white guy in an all-black Pentecostal church, speaking in tongues and praising Jesus. I was filled with the Holy Spirit and I had a whole new perspective on life.

I had found my family. The people I had never been around before were now my brothers and sisters. They felt closer to me than my own blood relatives! I stayed in that church for 8 years and grew in the Lord. My entire life changed, including all of my passions and desires. I have never been the same.

But still, I had questions.

After being saved, I spent 30 years working full-time in the secular world while also teaching adult Bible studies, serving as an assistant pastor, and doing other types of ministries. All the while, these questions plagued me, but they also became my new passion. These questions were like a thirst that demanded to be satisfied.

If you are like most Christians, you still have questions too. And it can be difficult to get a clear answer.

As a Spirit-filled, Bible-believing man of God, I believed in all the gifts of the Holy Spirit. Occasionally, someone would give a prophecy or an interpretation of tongues. There were times when God moved through me to give words of knowledge that proved accurate. I had received many revelations from the Lord, and had even seen visions.

But the thing I was not seeing was authentic and indisputable miracles that defied the laws of nature. It cannot be ignored that these types of supernatural events appear to have been a regular part of the life of the early church. Of course, I believed in miracles. I had heard stories of miracles happening in far-off places. Every now and then, I would even meet someone who had experienced a miracle. But I had not ever seen or experienced one myself.

THE EARLY CHURCH VERSUS TODAY'S CHURCH

However, this is not at all like the experience of the early church. Even back before Jesus went to the cross, He had given His followers power to heal the sick, cast out demons, and raise the dead. And contrary to a popular-but-false notion, it wasn't just for the apostles!

We read in Luke 10:1-12 that Jesus sent 72 others out, telling them to go ahead of Him into each town and preach the message that the kingdom of God is near. He also told them to heal *every* sick person they encountered.

Who were these people? Of the 72, we are not given a single name. All we know is that these were in addition to the 12 because chapter 9 starts out by telling us, "When Jesus had called the Twelve together, he gave them power and authority to drive out all demons and to cure diseases, and he sent them out to proclaim the kingdom of God and to heal the sick" (Luke 9:1-2 NIV).

Then chapter 10 begins by telling us of 72 "others" who were given power in addition to the 12: "After this the Lord appointed seventy-two others and sent them two by two ahead of him to every town and place where he was about to go" (Luke 10:1 NIV).

We know very little about them except that they were ordinary people who were drawn to Jesus. When Jesus asked them to join Him in His mission, they stepped up, answered the call, and went out in His name. And do you know what happened next? Miracles!

The sick were healed. Those suffering demonic

oppression were delivered. And many believed the message of the kingdom of God.

So clearly one did not have to be an apostle or in any other special club to receive miraculous power from Jesus. But what about the church today? What about the average believer who is filled with God's Holy Spirit? Where are the miracles in their lives? Those early disciples hadn't even been redeemed by the blood of the Lamb yet. They were not yet filled with the Holy Spirit, but miraculous signs and wonders confirmed the message they preached.

WHAT ABOUT YOU?

At some point, you have to come to the place of believing the Word of God over your own personal experiences. Jesus Christ said, "Very truly I tell you, whoever believes in me will do the works I have been doing, and they will do even greater things than these, because I am going to the Father" (John 14:12 NIV). I know I am not alone here. Perhaps just like me, you have wondered, "What am I missing, Lord? My life experiences don't match up with this description."

I hope you are also like me in this regard: I don't want to miss out on anything Jesus paid for and intended for me to have! For nearly 40 years now, I have searched for answers. The missing puzzle pieces. The hidden keys that would unlock doors to the miraculous.

Then one day, the answer came.

I did not have a visitation from any angel. There was no near-death experience where Jesus came and told me secret things at the foot of my hospital bed. I wasn't caught up to Heaven in a glorious vision. It was all much simpler than that.

Years ago, I received salvation through a bit of knowledge that I did not previously have. In the same manner, I began to walk in the miraculous after receiving a bit of knowledge and understanding that I had previously been missing. That's all it took—everything changed!

The Lord showed me that there were certain keys to walking in the miraculous. These keys are very simple biblical truths, but for some reason, our minds struggle to walk them out. We struggle, first to grasp these truths, and then later to live in them. But ever since that day when the Lord gave me understanding, I have prayed for thousands of people from all over the world and witnessed many miracles.

This book was written to pass on the knowledge I received from the Lord that day.

MIRACULOUS POWER IS AVAILABLE TO EVERY CHRISTIAN

Every Christian can walk in the miraculous, whether they've been saved for 20 years or 20 minutes. Healing, miracles, and deliverance are happening in a move of God that is cutting across the boundaries of race, culture, education, or denomination. And the importance of the movement cannot be overemphasized.

Just as it was in the days of the first disciples, the greatest tools for winning the lost to Christ are the Gospel backed up by a demonstration of God's miraculous power. I can tell you firsthand that when an atheist becomes the personal recipient of God's power, it's very difficult for them to remain an atheist!

Talk alone is cheap. When the world hears your message without a demonstration of God's power, it's very easy for them to dismiss it. This is how Paul described the issue:

> My message and my preaching were not with wise and persuasive words, but with a demonstration of the Spirit's power, so that your faith might not rest on human wisdom, but on God's power.
>
> — 1 CORINTHIANS 2:4-5 NIV

The keys outlined in this book will cause you to walk in closer intimacy with Jesus. You'll have a greater confidence in God's willingness to back you up when you step out in faith to pray for the lost. He will put greater compassion in your heart.

The keys exist.

They are available.

They work.

They are offered to everyone.

Many books make extraordinary claims and it's frustrating when they don't deliver. I don't claim to be anything special or spectacular. I'm just a regular

Christian like you. But since learning these truths and walking them out, I have taught them to many other Christians all over the world. The results are extraordinary. People are seeing book of Acts miracles when they begin to operate in these simple truths.

What about you? Are you ready for an adventure?

1

THE KEYS EXIST

Haley was in her early 30s, but she was using a walker to shuffle around much like an elderly person would. Haley suffered from a rare condition that caused severe arthritis throughout her body. She was in constant pain, and her range of motion was very limited. In addition to her inability to walk normally, Haley could not bend over at all.

In faith, I declared to Haley that if she would allow me to pray for her, that God would surely heal her and take away all of her pain.

There was just one "problem." I had never seen anyone healed before! My confidence did not come from previous experience. Rather, I was speaking out of pure faith. I was daring to believe that what Jesus says is true—that as a believer in Him, I was qualified and authorized to do the same works He did.

After I prayed for Haley, her range of motion fully

returned. She was shocked. But the good news did not stop there. All of the pain left her body. She was completely healed, and she has remained fully healthy to this day.

As surprised as Haley was, I'm sure I was even more so. This was the first time I saw someone miraculously healed through my ministry, and since that time, there have been thousands more. I have seen God bless many people, and have even seen atheists saved right on the spot after experiencing a healing miracle.

REACHING THE LOST WITH MIRACLES

After ministering to many lost and unchurched people, I have come to a firm conclusion. Most atheists are not actually atheists. Most of the time, there is a much deeper heart issue going on with them. Often, it's because they feel that God personally let them down at some point. Maybe they prayed for a certain person or situation and did not see the answer they wanted. Other times, they've seen too much evil and suffering and they decide that a good God would never allow such things.

But instead of truly believing that He doesn't exist, most of the time what they are doing is actively hating God or living in bitterness toward Him. When you talk to atheists while doing ministry, they often become very angry and passionate about their "disbelief." This betrays a fact that they really don't want to face. I'll try to explain using an illustration.

When I was a child, I used to believe in the tooth

fairy and in Santa Claus. In time, I grew up and realized that these were just mythical characters. They're not real. If you bring either of them up to me, I have no unresolved feelings about them. In my mind, they are dismissed as nonsense. I would not get angry talking about them. Why would I get angry at beings that do not exist?

However, atheists often express deep, passionate anger toward God—even while claiming that they don't believe He exists. Why would someone be angry at a "fairy tale"? Again, the real problem is an intense hatred of God. That's why the atheist often wants to do everything possible to discredit God and those who follow Him. Bitterness is often their underlying motivation, not a simple belief in the non-existence of God.

Many times, I have prayed for atheists that I first had to challenge in some way in order to receive their permission. They will say something like, "You can't heal me. I don't believe in that nonsense. There is no God!"

"Well then, here is a perfect opportunity for you to prove me wrong," I will respond. "I will pray for you and if nothing happens, you will prove that you were right and I was wrong!" Sometimes this challenge works and they will agree to let me pray for them. The atheist who does this often feels certain that nothing is going to happen. But when God shows up on the scene, everything changes.

Sometimes, they will appear to be in shock and will

ask for time to process what happened. Other times, they will openly acknowledge the miracle and I get to respond, "Isn't that amazing? The God you don't believe in just healed you! He must love you!" But often, the result is even more dramatic. Many times, when we go out and minister healing to a non-believer, we get to celebrate with all of Heaven. As much as I love ministering to God's people, my favorite healing miracles are the ones that involve a non-believer immediately becoming a Christian.

BOBBY

In the middle of a parking deck on a hot August day, Bobby caught my eye as he walked with a limp. His arms were well on their way to being covered with tattoos, he wore a backward baseball cap, sunglasses, and those round earrings that put large holes inside people's ears. Bobby was sporting a tank top that revealed his tattoos, but it also appeared to have satanic and occult symbols on it. The top of the shirt had the appearance of a Ouija board. There were crosses, flames, five-pointed stars, and other types of symbols, all sort of crowded around what looked like a large demonic face. At the bottom was the word, "Farewell."

I don't know what any of it was really supposed to mean, I just know that the One who is in me is greater than the one who is in the world. Bobby did not express belief of any kind in God or Jesus, but he did not seem hostile either. When I asked if he had any pain, Bobby indicated that he had significant pain in his feet and lower legs.

"So I'm going to pray for you and it's going to take all the pain away," I explained.

"Okay . . ." he responded with some hesitancy, but no resistance.

I said that if all the pain went away, that would be miraculous, and Bobby agreed. Then I explained more about the nature of what was about to take place.

"So I'm going to tell you why that's going to happen. It's going to happen because even if you don't know Him, Jesus loves you. He wants to take your pain away. That's what He does. Okay?"

"Okay."

Pointing at Bobby's legs, I prayed, "Father, in Jesus' name, I thank You for who You are, and I thank You for Bobby. And right now, I speak to Bobby's feet and his legs. And I command all the pain, get out. Right now. All of it."

I stood silently for a moment.

"Whoa," said Bobby.

"What are you feeling, Bobby?" He stood silent, staring at his legs. "What are you feeling?" I asked again.

"Well . . . I don't feel the pain *right now*," he explained with surprise in his voice.

"Move around and test it out," I suggested.

He began to walk, and I walked with him.

"Yeah, I was just limping . . ."

He continued to walk normally while adding, "Ten seconds ago, I was just limping and could barely walk."

"And now you can walk."

"Yeah, I feel like I could probably run right now."

"And you have no pain?" I asked.

"No, actually, I really don't feel the pain at all anymore."

Bobby was not a very excitable type of person, but you could tell he was somewhat shocked. I said, "You don't feel the pain anymore—isn't that cool?"

"That's . . . insane," he concluded.

At that moment, I began to share the Gospel with Bobby.

"That's because Jesus loves you, Bobby, even if you don't know Him."

"Whoa," Bobby said again. Maybe he was just as surprised to hear that as he was that the pain was gone.

I explained, "I won't twist your arm because I don't do that kind of stuff, okay? But Jesus wants to be part of your life. He wants to save you and make you a brand-new person . . ." As I shared the Gospel with Bobby, he looked down at the ground, his mouth open, as if he were feeling very surprised by what was taking place. I finished my Gospel presentation by asking, "Would you be interested in having Jesus come into your heart?"

"Yeah," was his immediate response.

We moved over a bit to get out of the way of passing cars, and then I led Bobby through a prayer of salvation.

"Heavenly Father . . ."

"Heavenly Father . . ."

"I know I'm a sinner."

"I know I'm a sinner." Bobby repeated with earnestness in his voice.

"And I know I need the Savior."

"And I know I need the Savior."

"And I believe Jesus is the Savior."

"And I believe Jesus is the Savior."

Slowly and peacefully, I guided Bobby through the process of receiving Christ as his Savior.

"So, Jesus . . ."

"So, Jesus . . ."

"Right now . . ."

"Right now . . ." Bobby's voice began to quiver.

"I repent for my sins."

"I repent for my sins." Bobby got a little clearer on that part, as if emphasizing his wholehearted agreement.

"And I ask you to forgive me for my sins."

"And I ask you to forgive me . . . for my sins." Bobby was starting to choke up a little at this point.

"And I ask You to come into my heart right now."

"And I ask You to come into my heart . . . right now."

"And be the Lord of my life."

"And be the Lord of my life." At that moment, tears began streaming down Bobby's face. You could feel his emotion.

"I give You my whole life right now."

"I give You my whole life right now," Bobby confessed, wiping the tears away.

"And I live my life for You."

Pausing just long enough to compose himself, Bobby continued, "And I live my life for You."

"Thank You for saving me."

With deep gratitude in his voice, Bobby concluded his prayer of salvation, "Thank You for saving me."

"In Jesus' name, Amen."

"In Jesus' name."

"Amen!"

I explained to Bobby that Jesus just came into his life and was filling him with light, peace, and love. "Jesus loves you, man. He loves you more than anyone has ever loved you. And He wants to give you a brand-new start—give you a brand-new life."

As Bobby continued to wipe the tears away from his face, I asked, "What does that feel like?"

"It feels *real*."

I was sharing in his joy and wanted to know more. I asked again, "What do you feel like?" His next words were very revealing.

"I feel like a new person," Bobby confessed.

Not 10 minutes before this, Bobby didn't know a thing about Jesus. He was just headed along in life as most people are, not thinking anything about his eternal destiny. One little healing later, and Bobby was a brand-new person.

The fields are ripe for harvest.

Lost people are out there just waiting, practically begging for someone to show them that God is real. That He loves them. That He wants them in His family.

There are so many people waiting for you to fulfill your assignment. Will you step up to the plate? Will you do the very simple things that need to be done to reach people like Bobby? Like Jaden?

JADEN

One time, I was out doing ministry and I came upon a group of young men who were playing Pokémon Go, a game in which people roam public places looking to pick up Pokémon creatures inside an app on their phones. I walked up to these young men and asked if they believed in miracles, and if so, where do they believe miracles come from? Several of the young men said that they do believe in miracles and that God is the source. Then there was Jaden.

Jaden did not believe in God or in anything supernatural. I said, "So where do you think miracles come from then?"

"From hard work and perseverance," he responded.

Next, I asked the entire group if any of them had any pain. Several of them did have pain, so I demonstrated God's healing power to them. The ones who had been healed were amazed and thankful. Then there was Jaden.

He had seen what was happening with the others, and he seemed interested. But he wasn't convinced. Probing further, I learned that Jaden was suffering from a sprained ankle. His pain was not debilitating, but it was pretty serious. At that point, I asked Jaden if I could pray for God to heal him.

He was skeptical, but he politely agreed to let me pray for him.

I explained that I would not even touch him. I would simply put the shadow of my hand over his ankle and pray. I did so, and then asked Jaden, "What are you feeling?"

He seemed very surprised and responded, "Something moved in my ankle."

I told him to test the ankle and see if there was any pain. At that point, Jaden was completely shocked. He shouted loudly to his friends, "No! That's not possible! It's gone! It's completely gone! The pain is *all* gone!"

After Jaden's experience, there were a few others to pray for. They all experienced healing and at that point, I began to explain the reason for the healing.

"Jesus is alive and well. He set up this encounter with you all today so that you could see a demonstration of His healing power. He did that because He loves you and wants to save you. He wants to have a personal relationship with each one of you. Jesus died on a cross to save you from your sins because He loves you and wants you to live in Heaven with Him forever. He wants you to be part of His family."

Then I asked, "Do any of you want to ask Jesus to come into your heart and save you today? Are you willing to turn away from a life of sin and serve Jesus instead?"

At that moment, Jaden gave an enthusiastic "Yes!" I

immediately led him in a prayer of repentance and dedication to Jesus. The young man who did not believe in God at all just a few moments prior was now a born-again child of God!

Healing isn't just about healing.

Prophecy isn't just about prophecy.

Miracles aren't just for the sake of the miracles.

All of these wonderful workings of God are for the purpose of demonstrating His love and His power to people. God wants the lost to know His goodness so that He can lead them into a relationship with our Savior Jesus Christ. And when we step out to minister, He will show up.

I believe that most Christians would love to see God's kingdom advancing in this way. Imagine if every Christian in the United States began venturing out to invade the spiritual darkness with God's light and love. We can do it! I spent years doing the regular church thing, but now I see God moving on a regular basis to save people, heal people, and bless people in all kinds of amazing ways.

Yes, God's supernatural power showed up in my ministry. Unfortunately, it came after a long period of me wrestling through various doubts.

WE ALL HAVE QUESTIONS

Questions will always arise in the heart when we are endeavoring to walk in the supernatural things of God. For example, some of the most common questions people struggle with are: Does this line up with the character of Christ? Could I imagine Jesus doing this?

Is this really something God intends for me to do, or is it only for a select few?

Do I have authority to do this whenever I want to, or should I only do it when God specifically tells me to do it?

Before I could walk in manifestations of the Spirit, I had to know that they were still in existence today, and that they were given to me for the purpose of advancing God's kingdom.

If you come from a cessationist background (i.e., a belief that the gifts of the Holy Spirit stopped after the death of the Apostles), then you will not believe that these signs and wonders are for today, nor will you believe that they are for you to use. Fortunately for me, I had met people who had experienced things that no doctor or scientist could explain through natural means. God had also allowed me to personally witness many manifestations of the supernatural gifts of the Holy Spirit, as everyday Christians operated in them. There were also the many books by people who operated in the realm of miraculous signs and wonders.

However, when I tried to step out in faith to see signs, wonders, healings, and other miracles, most of the time nothing would happen.

GOD'S TRUTH VERSUS PERSONAL EXPERIENCE

If I had gone strictly by my own personal experience, I would undoubtedly have concluded that miracles are not for today. That the supernatural was only for the early church. That God no longer works this way.

But I could not believe those things. I knew better. There were too many valid testimonies of people who were experiencing the same kinds of miracles the early church experienced. Miracles have not ceased. There was also the plain teaching of God's Word. Remember, Jesus said that "whoever believes" in Him would do the same works He did, and even greater works.

So that must have meant the problem was with me!

Jesus stated another important truth, or principle, several times in Scripture. "According to your faith let it be done to you" (Matthew 9:29 NIV). Matthew 8:13 (ESV) records Jesus saying to the centurion, "Go; let it be done for you as you have believed." Over and over Jesus tells people that they are healed through their faith.

If you are putting your faith in the idea that miracles are not for today, then you will receive results that line up with your belief. "According to your faith" it will be done for you, so you will probably not see any miracles. However, this does not prove that miracles are not for today. It only proves that you have received in accordance with what you believed.

Knowing that God was still performing miracles on the earth today, I felt confident that I had satisfactorily .

worked through this issue. My faith said that Jesus Christ was still doing miracles on the earth today. They have not ceased.

That left me with another important question.

ARE MIRACLES FOR ME?

Once we recognize that God is still performing miracles just like He always has, we're left to wonder: Am I supposed to walk in miracles? Are they for me? We don't need to rely on personal experience for the answer. Just as we did with the last question, we can rely on the Word of God as our measuring stick for truth. Here's what God's word says about this topic:

> Very truly I tell you, **whoever believes in me** will do the works I have been doing, and they will do even greater things than these, because I am going to the Father.

> — JOHN 14:12 NIV, EMPHASIS ADDED

Yes, we're going to see this verse many times because it imparts an extremely important truth. Jesus even starts out the verse by basically saying, "Look, I'm not lying to you. I'm telling you the truth here!" Then He goes on to explain that "whoever believes in me" will do the works He had been doing. What works had He been doing? Healing miracles. Casting out demons. Raising the dead.

Jesus did not say that only a select group of believers would do these things. He did not say that only believers who lived in a certain time period would do these things. He stated plainly and truthfully that "whoever" believes in Him would do these things.

That includes you.

That includes me.

Once I came into agreement with this simple truth, miracles began to happen in my ministry.

When the Lord first opened my eyes to the truth that miracles were available to me in my ministry, it still seemed like a theory. I had not tested it yet. However, I wasn't going to wait around. The same day God opened my eyes to this truth is the same day I went out and looked for someone to pray for. As soon as I saw Haley, it was obvious she was in serious need of healing. Praise God, He healed her that day right on the spot, and ever since then, I've been able to witness His miracles over and over.

But perhaps the most compelling part is that after I began to teach these principles to others, they had the same kind of experience. Once they received the truth that miracles are for today, and for them, they experienced similar results. Just like me, the people I've taught have seen miracle after miracle after miracle.

What kind of miracles, you might ask? They include blind eyes seeing and deaf ears hearing. Cancer vanishing. Broken bones being instantly healed and restored as though they had never been broken. Tumors disappearing.

People who could barely move having their full range of motion restored.

Heart problems healed.

Kidney problems healed.

Fertility problems gone.

The list goes on, and I'll share more testimonies throughout the book. But for now, I'd like to tell you about Alberto.

A MANGLED LEG IS RESTORED

Shortly after seeing my first successes in praying for the miraculous, a group of people from our church traveled to Mexico. There was a mission trip that had been planned by others, and late during the planning, I decided to go along.

We got there and our primary objective was to help an orphanage in Tecate for several days. After working at the orphanage each day, we would go out into the nearby villages for personal ministry. Many of the homes in these communities had no running water, so we took a large water truck with us and offered to fill the barrels of anyone who needed water. While we were giving out the water, we would also, through an interpreter, ask if anyone in the household needed prayer.

One of the small shacks we walked up to had a crude front porch area and the whole family had gathered there. After we asked if anyone in their house needed prayer, the father of the home, Alberto, emerged and stated that he was in desperate need. He had just been hired to work in a local factory and was supposed to start the next day. This new job was incredibly important to his family because they were extremely poor. But Alberto had a huge problem.

Alberto stated that he had suffered from an injury, and he didn't think he was going to be able to stand for a full day of work. I asked him exactly what the problem was and he pulled up his pant leg. What he showed us was nothing short of gruesome.

Alberto's leg and foot had been completely mangled. His calf had several deep grooves going from his knee to his ankle. It looked as if a bear or a lion had simply ripped through his leg with its claws, removing huge chunks of flesh along the way. The leg looked to have been left without any kind of professional medical treatment. Skin seems to have grown back over the gaping wounds.

Besides that, his foot was completely twisted, pointing out to the side instead of straight ahead. He could not move the foot into a straightened position. It was permanently locked sideways. His leg was twisted and mangled, and all of this together made him lean drastically to one side when he stood up. As if all of that weren't enough, Alberto's pain was severe and constant. We asked him to rate the pain he was feeling in that moment on a scale of 1-10, and he indicated it was a 9.

Remember, I had only recently begun seeing the miraculous in my ministry. Everyone in our group was pretty much brand new to pursuing healing and other miracles. But before I even realized what was coming out of my mouth, I stated confidently to the interpreter: "Tell him that I will pray for him right now, and his leg will grow back normal. His foot will become straight. And all of his pain will go."

One of the women from my church looked at me with a look of horror in her eyes. She looked both shocked and angry at me for having said this. Then she basically let me know that her disapproval was out of fear that Alberto would be severely disappointed if nothing happened.

For some reason though, I was so full of faith that I was completely undeterred. I asked everyone to gather around and watch closely so that I could teach them how to pray for the injury.

At that point, I had Alberto sit down. I took both of his ankles in my hands, and I was just getting ready to loudly command a miracle. Before I got a single word out of my mouth, Alberto's leg shot out straight. His foot turned straight and all of his pain was completely gone. There were still scars, but his leg and foot became completely functional again—instantaneously.

I remember being a little disappointed that I didn't get to show everyone how to pray for healing. Of course, I quickly got over that. Alberto's entire family erupted into cheers and praise to Jesus. We all cried tears of joy as we watched God's goodness being poured out on this family that had been in desperate need.

The woman who had been upset with me that day had been raised in a denomination that taught cessationism, and up until that miraculous moment, she still did not believe that miracles were for today. However, from that day on, she understood that not only are miracles for today, they are for "whoever believes." She has now prayed for many people herself, and has witnessed many miraculous healings as a result.

You can do the same. We just have to work on what you believe, and what you know.

2

THE NATURE OF THE KEYS

People from all over the world just show up at the doorstep of our church on Thursdays for our Marketplace Ministry training. One week, a man named Chris showed up and went out with us. I was able to train him in ministering the miraculous to strangers in public, and he was so impacted by the experience that he came back to our church about a month later.

This time, Chris had come to one of our Sunday morning services. We have two services on Sunday mornings, and I have about a 15-minute window between the first and second service. Chris approached me during that time and said he had brought some friends who were in need of healing. Chris got right to the point and asked if I could take some time to pray for them.

I felt a little rushed. Honestly, I was not really feeling "into it" at all. Explaining that I only had a few moments, I said I would pray quickly for them and then I would have to leave. They understood and agreed.

The prayer time was so fast that I struggled to recall very much of it when a man named Scott called me about a month later and asked if I remembered him. Scott explained that I had prayed for him, his wife, Tanya, and Shinelle, his niece. Then Scott said he wanted to take me to lunch to tell me what happened. I agreed, and then went to meet Scott and Shinelle to listen to their story.

As we sat waiting for our food, Scott asked if I remembered the different issues we had prayed over. I explained that it was all a blur in my mind. Then he asked, "Do you remember praying for Tanya's breast cancer?" Honestly, I did not remember. Then Scott explained, "You had her place her hand on the location of the tumor. Then you touched her hand and told the cancer to go. You instructed Tanya to go and have a doctor check it out. We did that, and she has no trace of cancer anywhere in her body!"

"Wow! Praise God! Thank you for sharing that wonderful testimony," I responded.

Scott said, "There's a lot more!" He continued, "Tanya fell off of a horse when she was a teenager and injured her back. She has been taking 15 Vicodin every day for over a decade to try to deal with the chronic pain. You prayed a simple prayer over her back, and she was healed. She has not had any pain since we left the church that day. She has not taken a single Vicodin, and get this—she never even had any kind of withdrawals!"

"Wow! God is good . . ." I responded, before Scott interjected again.

"There's more!" he exclaimed.

Scott continued to relay every detail and I listened excitedly. I may not have been "into" the prayer time in between services that day, but the results were riveting.

Scott asked, "Do you remember that I told you I had lower back problems, and how you responded?"

"No, I don't. What did I say?"

"You told my wife that the problem was with my legs. You told her to hold up my legs and pray over them. You told her what to pray, word for word, and when she did, I was healed from that time forward. What was interesting was that my wife has never prayed for anyone publicly, and has never felt comfortable doing that. Of course you didn't know that. Well, this time she did pray, and I was healed!"

Once again, I was quite surprised and thankful for what God had done. But it's what he said next that really blew me away.

"Do you remember praying for my kidney?"

"No, sorry. Not really." I honestly still could not recall any of the details of our brief prayer time that day.

Scott explained, "I had been suffering from kidney disease and was in regular need of dialysis. Eventually, both of my kidneys shut down and died. My only hope for living a normal life was to get a transplant from a donor. Eventually, we discovered that my wife's brother was a match, so he donated one of his kidneys to me several months before you prayed with us that day. I asked you to pray that everything would work out and that my body would not reject the new kidney."

"And I'm not sure why, but then I mentioned that the two dead kidneys were still inside my body because that is the normal procedure—to leave them in as long as they aren't causing any other problems. You immediately responded, 'How about bringing those two kidneys back to life?' And after asking that question, you just commanded them to be restored."

As I listened, I felt certain that Scott was about to tell me that his body was now doing fine because the new kidney was working perfectly and his body had not rejected it.

But that's not what he said.

"I went back to my doctor to have my kidney checked out and something really bizarre happened. The doctor told me that *all three kidneys* are now functioning perfectly! The two dead ones came back to life!"

Scott went on to explain that there is a nationwide network of doctors who share information about kidney transplant recipients. They post the results of the chemical analysis of the urine of those patients, which tells the doctors how well the kidneys are functioning. Scott's numbers were the best in the country!

You can find Scott sharing a brief version of his testimony on my YouTube channel. The title of the video is: *Scott Hoeck, THREE KIDNEY MIRACLE!!! – Tom Loud.*

What's so interesting to me about this particular set

of miracles is that it didn't matter how I felt that day. Our access to kingdom power is not based on a feeling. And as you can tell from my reaction to Scott telling his story, the results really weren't based on my personal level of belief. It's not that I'm personally convinced about the specific outcome of any particular situation I face. There are simply some things I know to be true because the Bible says they are true.

KNOWLEDGE OF THE KEYS

The keys to unlocking kingdom power are all tied to knowledge. Knowledge carries a far greater weight than simple "belief." Knowledge is not a theory, not a supposition, and not even a product of blind faith. Rather, knowledge is indisputable fact.

Think about it this way: Truth doesn't change based on someone's beliefs. Truth is true whether someone believes it to be true or not. So ask yourself the following: Who actually knows the truth about all things?

There is only one right answer to this question, of course. God is the only eyewitness to every event that has ever occurred. The only insider to every secret that has ever been kept. The only creator and designer of everything that exists. The one who knows and understands every law of nature, because He's the One who wrote them. Jesus Christ alone!

Okay, so this One who knows everything, He doesn't keep all of His knowledge to Himself. He shares many things with us. In fact, He has written a book that He gave to man. The Bible is God communicating truth to us. If we are going to build our faith on anything, let's build it on God's Word—which cannot be shaken, moved, or changed in any way. Let's not believe what the pastors, the scholars, the rabbis, or the priests have to say. Let's throw out man's opinions and ideas, and let's agree that what we can *know* for sure is what God tells us to be true.

When what you believe disagrees with what God's Word has plainly stated, then it's certain that your belief is incorrect. So what else, exactly, does Jesus say about the people who believe in Him?

> And these signs will accompany those who believe: In My name they will drive out demons; they will speak in new tongues; they will pick up snakes with their hands, and if they drink any deadly poison, it will not harm them; they will lay their hands on the sick, and they will be made well.
>
> — MARK 16:17-18 BSB

If you are a true believer, then these words must apply to you.

And now we've identified what the keys to unlocking kingdom power actually are—they are simply truths of God that need to be correctly understood, believed, and applied. Right now, you—as a born-again Christian—already have all the keys you will ever need to unlock the kingdom power within you.

THE KEYS MUST BE USED

Say you possessed a key to a gate that held great riches on the other side. If you never used that key, you'd be missing out. But why would anyone have the key that unlocks great wealth, but never use it? The only rational responses would be, "Because they did not know they had the key." Or, "They did not understand what the key was." You could have something in your possession but still not understand what it is, or what it is for. Without the proper knowledge, the key would not be very useful. However, with the proper knowledge, the key is very useful.

I recently went through this exact scenario in real life. I found a key in the pocket of an old jacket. However, I had no idea what the key went to, so I actually went around trying it. I checked various doors in our church and our home, all to no avail. The key is not useful to me right now, but the fact remains that it does have the power to unlock a door somewhere.

Whether you believe it yet or not, you have all the keys within you to unlock everything pertaining to the kingdom of God. The keys dwell within you as a believer of Jesus Christ. Interestingly enough, Jesus actually said that He would give to His followers, "the keys to the kingdom of Heaven."

At the time He spoke this truth, He had not yet paid

the ultimate price for the sins of humankind. He was speaking about something that would take effect after He finished His work of redemption on the cross. That's why He didn't say, "I have given you . . ." He said, "I will give you . . ."

We who have received Christ in our hearts are living in the post-Cross era. Everything humankind was waiting for, which could only be accomplished by the Messiah, is here now. We can now say along with Jesus, "It is finished!" We are no longer waiting to receive the keys to the kingdom of Heaven. They are here for all who believe.

He has finished the work the Father sent Him to accomplish. Then He called us, equipped us, and gave us the ministry of reconciliation in this world. It is our mission to reconcile people to God by preaching the Gospel and demonstrating God's power as a witness to the truth of that Gospel. We are not waiting for some distant future to receive the keys to the kingdom of God. We have them.

Jesus did His part. He promised to give us the keys, and He fulfilled that promise. But it is up to us to recognize this reality and then use the keys as God intends.

The full verse in Matthew explains it this way: "I will give you the keys of the kingdom of heaven; whatever you bind on earth will be bound in heaven, and whatever you loose on earth will be loosed in heaven" (Matthew 16:19 NIV). In that verse, Jesus says plainly that He will give us the keys to the kingdom of

Heaven, but that verse does not tell us how to use the keys. So that's what we need to learn. How do we use these keys to help usher people into God's kingdom? This can only be accomplished once we gain a clearer understanding of how God's kingdom works.

Just like the natural world is governed by natural laws, there are laws in place in the spirit realm. If I'm going to live by the spirit and operate according to the rules of the spirit realm, then I need a clear understanding of those rules.

THE SPIRIT REALM

The first thing to understand is that the rules or "laws" of the spirit realm are different from the laws of the natural realm. Some of the differences are obvious. God and His angels aren't constrained by time and space the way we are. They seem to have the ability to become visible to the natural world at times, while most of the time remaining invisible. But whether visible or invisible, the spirit world is always interacting with and impacting the natural world.

Because the spirit realm is invisible to us, we have a tendency to think of it as being "less real." However, if we truly ponder the case for existence, we would have to conclude that the spirit realm is more "real"—if there is such a thing. The reason being that the spirit realm is eternal. Everything we see is temporary. Almost like a shadow.

The spirit realm, on the other hand, will exist

forever. It is eternal. The spirit realm is an exciting place to consider. But it is also very difficult for us to grasp because it is different from the natural world—the only world we've ever known.

Understanding the spirit realm is more like putting together a jigsaw puzzle than it is building a house. If you were building a house, you'd need to know exactly which materials to start with. But when putting together a jigsaw puzzle, you can start with any piece. The order you put them together doesn't matter so much as long as you have all the pieces and eventually put them in the right place.

Once you understand all of the keys, you'll be able to assemble the puzzle and the picture will become very clear.

WHERE ARE THE KEYS?

Now when He was asked by the Pharisees when the kingdom of God would come, He answered them and said, "The kingdom of God does not come with observation; nor will they say, 'See here!' or 'See there!' For indeed, the kingdom of God is within you."

— LUKE 17:20-21 NKJV

All the gifts of the Spirit are in you right now because the Holy Spirit is within you. When the Holy

Spirit makes His home in you, He doesn't come empty-handed. He brings all of his gifts with Him. Isn't this very straightforward logic?

It's a wonder that we struggle to grasp it. The Holy Spirit is living within us and that means all of His supernatural power resides there with Him. That power just needs to be uncovered, or maybe we should say "discovered."

When you begin to discover what resides within you because of Who resides within you, then you can begin to walk in kingdom power! My goal is that every born-again believer would walk in the fullness of everything God has given to us, His children. However, we must desire and be willing to walk in that power. We must want to see the power of His kingdom opening up the watchful eyes of a lost and dying world. The ones who are desperately looking for evidence that God is alive and well and active in the world today.

We must desire that goal more than our own personal comfort, doubts, insecurities, or anything else that might seek to get in the way.

3

THE KEY OF IDENTITY

Our identity in Christ is paramount to everything we do and everything we believe. Think about this: Your opinion will never carry the same weight as God's assessment. God assesses and rightly judges each and every person, situation, or thing. He's never wrong. He has complete and perfect understanding. The rest of us mostly have opinions.

My opinions, your opinions, and other people's opinions will never carry the weight of God's perfect understanding. But often we challenge what God says about who we are. Sometimes we see ourselves as unclean. Powerless. Victims. Mere mortals. There are a thousand other possible limitations and weaknesses we place on ourselves in our own minds and hearts. But the truth about who we are is found in what God thinks and says about us. It's His view that is accurate, not ours. Not anyone else's.

So who are you, according to God's view?
You are the righteousness of God.

God made him who had no sin to be sin for us, so that in him **we might become the righteousness of God**.

> — 2 CORINTHIANS 5:21 NIV, EMPHASIS ADDED

You are not defeated. You are a conqueror.

No, in all these things **we are more than conquerors** through him who loved us.

> — ROMANS 8:37 NIV, EMPHASIS ADDED

You are a member of God's household.

Consequently, you are no longer foreigners and strangers, but fellow citizens with God's people and also **members of his household**.

> — EPHESIANS 2:19 NIV, EMPHASIS ADDED

Jesus Christ was the Son of God. His status as "Son" is what enabled Him to do the amazing works he did. But how does God see you? What is your status?

> Behold, what manner of love the Father hath bestowed upon us, **that we should be called the sons of God**.

> — 1 JOHN 3:1 KJV, EMPHASIS ADDED

You are a son of God. We can often view ourselves as beggars, living off of scraps that fall from God's table. But that is not at all how God sees us.

> To Him who loved us and washed us from our sins in His own blood, and **has made us kings and priests to His God and Father**, to Him be glory and dominion forever and ever. Amen.

> — REVELATION 1:5-6 NKJV, EMPHASIS ADDED

We could keep going, as there are many more verses in the Bible that tell us what God really thinks about us. But the point right now is to recognize that the way you think about yourself is probably a lot different from the way God thinks about you. I don't walk around in my daily life thinking of myself as a king. You probably don't either.

But as a child of God, that's what you are. You are royalty. And the spirit realm recognizes that authority. The issue is whether or not you recognize it. Think about it this way. Say there is a certain kingdom. The king has many wives and therefore many children.

The children of the king have special rights and privileges. But even more important than that, they have authority. When people come into the presence of a prince, they bow down. They don't argue. They don't challenge. They definitely don't fight.

Now, what if one of those princes didn't understand who he was? Say he lost his memory and he is living out among the common people. He's wearing common clothes and working a normal job, paying rent, paying taxes, and putting up with his boss. Worse than that, there are deceivers about who are taking advantage of the prince. These people hate the king and the kingdom. They know who the prince really is, but since he doesn't know, they enjoy doing things that harm him. And they're just going to keep doing that. They're not going to recognize and acknowledge his authority.

Why?

Because he himself doesn't recognize it. So why would they? If the prince doesn't recognize who he is and the power he has, they certainly aren't going to tell him. Instead, they will just keep taking advantage of him and trampling on him.

But as soon as that prince comes into an understanding of who he is—his true identity—everything changes. The prince takes his rightful place in the kingdom. He puts on his royal robes, takes his seat on a throne, and begins to give commands that have the weight of law. What will those same people do now? Will they obey the commands of the prince?

You bet they will. They have to. They don't even have a choice.

And that's how it is with the enemy. Once we recognize who we are in Christ, it's all over for the devil. You have the authority of a king. You have the spiritual status of a priest. God says that you carry the same power and authority that Jesus demonstrated while He was on the earth.

Understanding who we are in God's eyes is what allows us to walk in confident authority. We encounter the enemy more often than we probably realize. The Bible teaches us that whenever someone is in unbelief, the enemy is holding them captive. God didn't create sickness, and it doesn't come from Him. In fact, He told His people even in Old Testament times that He would "take away all sickness" from among them if they would simply obey His commands.

Now that we've become the righteousness of God through Jesus Christ, that requirement has been fulfilled. We just get to enjoy the benefit! So when we encounter sickness, we are able to take authority over it. Just like Jesus encountered people who were oppressed, enslaved, blind, or living in fear and hopelessness, we encounter those same strongholds of the enemy and we have the power to liberate people. Just like Jesus did, we have the Holy Spirit living inside of us, and that means we have everything necessary to meet people's needs.

CALLED AND EQUIPPED

As God's sons and daughters, we don't just have the ability to meet people's needs for healing, deliverance, and provision. We have the responsibility to do those things. Just like the Father called Jesus to demonstrate His power so that the Father would be glorified, we are called to do the same.

You are called by God to do the same things Jesus did.

Several years ago, I was teaching in London when a woman from India came up and explained that she had come to see me because she knew that if I prayed for her, she would receive the impartation of the gift of speaking in other tongues. *Okay, this is different,* I thought to myself.

Honestly, I don't know whether I truly believed I could impart this special gift to her or not. There seemed to be some doubt. But I set aside my own thoughts and opinions, and instead went to God's truth. "Whatever the need, the Father has equipped me as His son to fill it," I told myself. Then I laid my hands on her and believed that God would meet the need just as He would if Jesus Himself was laying His hands on this lady.

This was beyond my personal experience. It was not something I had ever done. But I just let God be God, acting through me, and sure enough the lady received exactly what she came for.

If Jesus never met a challenge that He could not

overcome, then Jesus living in you should also never meet a challenge that cannot be overcome. When you realize what God's Word says about you is who you really are, and what God says you can do is what you can actually do, then you can begin to operate in the fullness of power that God has made available to all of His children.

IDENTITY DETERMINES RIGHTS

Citizenship matters. Think about this. If someone is a US citizen and they travel abroad, does that mean they cease to be a citizen? Did they give up their citizenship for a time? No, definitely not. And there are benefits to that citizenship. If war breaks out or there is some other type of problem, the US citizen can go find refuge at the US Embassy located in that country.

You've probably seen the movies where a US citizen gets into trouble with the local authorities. As they are being chased by the authorities of that land, they run up toward the gate of the embassy yelling "US citizen!" The Marines guarding the gate open it just enough to let the US citizen pass through, and they slam it shut just before the "bad guys" can get through. That's it. The fight is over. The local authorities have no power or authority to cross the gate and get the US citizen.

Where is your citizenship?

Philippians 3:20 tells us that if we are saved, we are citizens of Heaven!

We're not in Heaven right now, but we are still full-fledged citizens with all of the rights and privileges that come along with that. We are citizens of the highest and most powerful kingdom in the entire universe!

I'd like to tell you about the process I underwent to become a US citizen. It was very long and hard. Are you ready?

I was born here.

Obviously, I'm kidding about the process being long and hard. I did nothing to earn my citizenship. I was born into it. When we are born again, we are immediately conferred with full citizenship in Heaven. We don't have to do anything to earn any of our rights.

When I was a baby, I had all the rights of a US citizen. I had them the moment I was born, and that's exactly how it is in the kingdom of God. You don't have to work your way up to some point where you finally receive your rights. You have them from the very beginning!

The devil obviously doesn't want us to know this or understand the implications of it. Because basically, the implication is that we don't have to put up with his garbage!

So he does everything he can to keep us in the dark on this. That is how he seeks to keep control, even over people who have kingdom power and authority. He cannot actually take power from them because he doesn't have the authority to do that. But what he does —and it's very effective—is to lie to us. He is constantly working to deceive those who have rights, power, and authority into thinking they don't have those things. That's why it's so very important to fully grasp our identity in Christ!

Perhaps you've heard the story about elephants in Thailand. The story goes that for centuries, elephants have been used as beasts of burden in Thailand. Instead of a bulldozer or a forklift, the local people there have historically used elephants to harvest the valuable teak trees from the jungle. The elephants are critically valuable to the industry, and sometimes the workers must go out into the jungle to capture a young wild elephant. Of course, that wild elephant will need to be tamed and trained to submit to its human masters.

When a wild elephant is first caught, it is understandably not very cooperative. It doesn't want to be tamed or trained. So the handlers will chain one of the young elephant's rear legs to a very flexible tree. In an attempt to get free, the elephant will start to pull on that chain. He will pull and pull with all of his might, then he'll pull some more. As he yanks that chain, it becomes tighter and tighter around his ankle, cutting into his skin and making his leg very sore.

As the soreness around his leg gets worse, he will still pull, but with less force. Then a little less. Then less.

After a while, the elephant finally stops pulling. He has learned that he cannot break the chain, and he accepts his defeat.

Once that day finally comes, the elephant is ready to be put to work. He can now be used by his masters to harvest teak trees. His handler can lead him around with a simple rope, and he will follow and obey. He will not try to run away. Why?

Because the chain is still around his leg.

It's not attached to anything on the other side. But the elephant still believes that escape is not possible, so he will not even try. He's actually free. He could walk away at any time. But he believes he is a captive, and that's what keeps him held captive.

This is exactly what happens to many Christians. When we become born again, the chain is broken. But the enemy comes along and says, "You're still captive. You're still mine. I've got you. You have no power to escape."

We look down at the chain around our ankle and say, "Yep, sure enough, he's right. I'm still a prisoner. If I try to fight, it will only end in defeat."

The enemy will attempt to blind our eyes to what we possess. He wants to keep our identity in the dark. He wants to darken and blur the truth about our identity as it is revealed in God's Word. If he is successful, he'll have us groping around blindly, in the dark, saying, "I guess I don't have it."

Don't let him do that to you, friend. I need you to dig down deep right now and get determined. Decide that you aren't going to let him do that to you or anyone else from this point forward. Determine that you are going to walk in the fullness of who you are in Christ.

Determine that you are going to finish this book all the way to the end.

Determine that you are going to fully grasp the truth of God's Word that is outlined in this book.

Go all in.

IDENTITY DETERMINES AUTHORITY

The word "power" in the New Testament has been translated from a couple of different Greek words. *Exousia* speaks of power in the sense of authority that a given person possesses. If I said the President of the United States had a lot of power, I'd be talking about *exousia*. The other Greek word is *dunamis*. *Dunamis* speaks of power in the sense of dynamic energy. It's the same root word we use to get the English word "dynamite."

The President of the United States also has *dunamis* power, at least at his disposal. His *exousia* power gives him the authority to command and wield physical *dunamis* power like human muscle, military equipment, and military weapons.

Just like the President, God possesses both types of power. He has armies of angels at his disposal, and He also has the ability to physically subdue, harm, or destroy His enemies all on His own if He chooses.

What He has given us to use for operating in the spirit realm, at least primarily, is *exousia* power. When a child of God who understands their God-given authority speaks in faith, spiritual beings and spiritual realities will conform to the authoritative command. Then the physical reality will reflect what has taken place in the spirit realm. This happens without any physical exertion from the speaker. The child of God does not have to use physical force, at least not personally. Angels may or may not play a role in carrying out the command.

The child of God doesn't need to be privy to the details of how his or her command is carried out. A military general doesn't necessarily have to know the details of how his orders will be carried out when he gives them. He can simply say "bomb that enemy" or "take out that airstrip" or "destroy every road and bridge leading into that enemy stronghold" and someone else will carry out the command.

Everything in creation has been programmed to obey God's authority. Yes, God gives free will. He commands certain things and people can choose to obey or not obey. Fallen angels and demons have chosen to generally live in rebellion against God. They don't obey the general commands He has given all of us for how to live. But when there is a specific command of authority, they don't have a choice. They must obey.

When it comes to the enemy, you can think of him like a captured criminal. If a violent criminal is left alone to run free, he will live in disobedience and rebellion, wreaking havoc in people's lives. But when the FBI finds him and raids his house, he is bound and thrown into prison. He is subdued and forced into compliance. Even though he doesn't want to, he will now do what he is told. He has no other choice.

You are not the military soldier or the FBI agent in these scenarios. You are the director of the FBI! You are the President. You are the king and the priest. All you have to do is recognize your authority and issue the command. The armies of God are at your disposal. They are waiting for you to give orders.

WHY OUR IDENTITY MATTERS SO MUCH

God's will has not yet been fully accomplished in this world. Once everything has been restored and we're living in what the Bible calls "the new Heaven and the new earth," everyone will be living in perfect harmony with God's will. But for now, there is still rebellion everywhere. The effects of that rebellion are still with us, and the enemy's armies are still generally on the loose. They are running free and wreaking havoc in people's lives.

That's why God has commissioned us to heal the sick, cast out demons, work miracles, and preach His Word. His power is in the hands of His children. As His children, it's our responsibility to partner with Him and do the work of His kingdom.

He has given us fairly broad leeway in regard to how we exercise our authority. God wants us to use our judgment in any situation we encounter to accomplish His will. We are not perfect, but the good news is that we don't have to be. We are very imperfect vessels in this life, but God uses us anyway!

When I was first saved, I mainly read the King

James Version. In the KJV, 1 Corinthians 13:11-12 says, "For now we see through a glass, darkly; but then face to face: now I know in part; but then shall I know even as also I am known." Back then, I interpreted that verse to mean that we are allowed to look into the realm of the spirit as if we are looking through a dark and hazy pane of glass. I thought it meant that we couldn't fully see things right now the way we will one day when we're in Heaven. But that is actually not what this verse is about.

The Greek word translated as "glass" is *esoptron*. *Esoptron* actually refers to a mirror, not just a regular piece of glass. This brings quite a different meaning from the one I had originally understood. The verse is actually saying that we look into a mirror under dim lighting conditions.

We're looking into a mirror and what we see is not fully illuminated. The image is a little dark. The verse is not talking about the spirit realm at all. What does a mirror show us? It shows us ourselves!

We also know that the Bible likens itself to a mirror.

Anyone who listens to the word but does not do what it says is like someone who looks at his face in a mirror and, after looking at himself, goes away and immediately forgets what he looks like.

— JAMES 1:23-24 NIV

The Word of God is a mirror. It's God's mirror. This verse from James uses the same Greek word, *esoptron*, as the verse from 1 Corinthians. So what is the verse from 1 Corinthians talking about? It's talking about seeing yourself the way you actually are. God's mirror gives you the most accurate reflection of who you really are. It tells you how God really sees you, and His vision isn't distorted! He is the One who can see clearly. It's what He says about you that's true.

So when you look into what God's Word says about you, you will see who you really are. The passage in James also encourages us to be doers of the Word. It teaches that anyone who doesn't do what the Word says is not using the mirror very effectively.

So how can we best use the mirror of God's Word? Make sure we follow a lot of rules? No pants in church for the ladies? No hats inside, and no swear words?

Some people mistakenly believe that this Scripture in James is telling us to use the Word of God as some kind of inspection device. Instead of "mirror" they somehow read, "magnifying glass" and believe that the primary purpose of God's Word is to get us looking at all of our flaws. Seeing all the ways we don't measure up, so that we can work harder at avoiding all the things that are wrong.

God's rules are good and necessary, but they do not get to the heart of the matter. Likewise, focusing on our flaws is not the goal. Once we clearly see our sin, repent, and ask forgiveness, God doesn't want us to go around thinking about it anymore. He forgets it completely. If you look at the preaching and teaching of Jesus, you'll see that He does not recommend focusing on our own flaws in some unachievable pursuit of moral perfection. So how do we become doers of the Word?

The best way to be a doer of the Word is to advance God's kingdom just like Jesus did. By going out among the lost to tell them the good news and do good works. Meet their needs and introduce them to a Father that loves them. Liberate all who are oppressed by the devil. This is what Jesus encourages His followers to do.

In order to do that, we must deeply and fully understand who we are in Christ. The person who does not live according to their identity in Christ is not being diligent to live according to the Word. They look at the Word and get a glimpse of who they really are according to God, but then they do not go out and live according to what it says about them.

They lose their true identity and they become vulnerable to taking on a false identity imposed on them by the world, the devil, or even their own carnal mind.

Don't be a person who forgets what they see in the Word of God! Remember what it says about you.

GOD'S WORD IS TRUSTWORTHY

A mirror does not create the image we see when we look into it. The mirror simply reflects what's actually there. In other words, the mirror does not lie. It does not exaggerate. The mirror just tells it like it is by reflecting light.

Did you know that a mirror can reflect a beam of sunlight to a distance of up to five miles? But have you ever tried to reflect a beam of darkness? Darkness cannot be reflected. Truthfully, there is no such thing as a beam of darkness because darkness doesn't exist, at least not on its own. It has no physical properties. It cannot be measured. It cannot be channeled or corralled or used for any purpose.

Darkness is just the absence of light.

It's the absence of power.

And what does the Bible call Satan? The Bible calls him "the prince of darkness." We could say that the Bible calls him "the prince of the absence of power." Or the "prince of the absence of light."

And that would accurately communicate two things about him. He has no real power. The only "power" he has is delegated power. God has the real power. The other thing it communicates is that Satan is working constantly to try to keep humankind in the dark— meaning he is trying to keep us away from the light of God's Word!

He knows that if he can keep us from understanding and fully receiving what the Bible says about us, he can keep an upper hand. But he also fears you fully understanding what the Bible says about you. He knows that if you learn the truth of what God's Word says about who you are, he will be no match for you.

When the seventy-two disciples returned, they joyfully reported to him, "Lord, even the demons obey us when we use your name!"

The devil knows that when you walk in the spiritual realm with the full knowledge of who you are in Christ, his knee must bow. When you speak with kingdom authority, he's done. The enemy has nothing to stand against kingdom authority—no weapon, no power, no defense. Demons will actually fear you. Isn't that interesting? Most people think of demons as something to be afraid of, but the Bible teaches that the enemy will be afraid of us!

What God's Word says about you is what's true. The mirror does not lie.

THE NEW CREATION

The Bible tells us in 2 Corinthians 5:17 (NLT) that "anyone who belongs to Christ has become a new person. The old life is gone; a new life has begun!" The old life is not hanging around, gradually getting lesser and lesser. It's completely gone!

You were a sinner, but now you're a saint.

You were a slave, but now you're a king.

God has given a new script for your life—the Word of God—and He wants us to fully understand our new role. He desires for us to think and act according to what we actually are. Unfortunately, too many Christians think that they are still basically the same person they were before. They think that they are supposed to live better now, but they fail to grasp that their very essence has fundamentally changed. The old role has been written out of the play, but of course the enemy keeps trying to get us to play according to that old role. Sinner. Defeated. Conquered. Slave.

> That, however, is not the way of life you learned when you heard about Christ and were taught in him in accordance with the truth that is in Jesus. You were taught, with regard to your former way of life, to put off your old self, which is being corrupted by its deceitful desires; to be made new in the attitude of your minds; and to put on the new self, created to be like God in true righteousness and holiness.
>
> — EPHESIANS 4:20-24 NIV

It's so easy to forget that you are a new creation. The devil wants us to believe that we are still the same "old man." He tries to make that into an identity that we will never escape. Don't believe him. He's a liar. Believe what God's Word says about you. Agree with what He says.

He says you are a king. A priest. Not just a conqueror, but more than a conqueror. He says that you are a saint. His child. His son. His daughter. A full heir with all rights and privileges.

If you live like that isn't true, you are disagreeing with God. Some Christians make the mistake of thinking this is an issue of humility. Humility is considering other people more important than yourself. Humility is not agreeing with what the enemy says about you. In fact, if you disagree with what God says about you, that could be considered the height of pride.

Who are you to disagree with what He says?

Our God loves us and He shares His magnificent power and nature with us. The level and nature of His love for us is beyond our wildest imaginations. It's beyond anything we can conceive of.

God says that you are an amazing creation—His masterpiece. You are His beloved son or daughter. You're not just some random stranger that came in off the street and is wandering around in His house. You're part of the family. You have God's spiritual DNA running through your veins.

You have His power in you, and He has called you to use it for His kingdom. That's who you are. The Bible says it, so you must believe it.

> And He said to them, "Go into all the world and preach the gospel to every creature. He who believes and is baptized will be saved; but he who does not believe will be condemned. And these signs will follow those who believe: In My name they will cast out demons; they will speak with new tongues; they will take up serpents; and if they drink anything deadly, it will by no means hurt them; they will lay hands on the sick, and they will recover."

So then, after the Lord had spoken to them, He was received up into heaven, and sat down at the right hand of God. And they went out and preached everywhere, the Lord working with *them* and confirming the word through the accompanying signs. Amen.

— MARK 16:15-20 NKJV

4

THE KEY OF AUTHORITY

A demonic spirit manifested from one woman I was ministering to in Seattle. When I told the evil spirit to come out of the woman, it responded, "I don't have to. I have a right to be in her." Normally when people encounter such a response, they will start having a conversation with the demon. It usually goes something like this.

"What right do you have to be in this woman?"

The demon will often say something like, "She used tarot cards when she was younger." Or maybe, "She did a lot of sexual sins as a teenager." Whatever the answer, it's usually based on something the person participated in or maybe somewhere they had been. This kind of conversation can go back and forth for quite a while if you allow it. But there's another option.

When this evil spirit told me that it wasn't going to leave because it had a right to be in this lady, I let the spirit know who I was and the authority I had. I responded, "You are a liar and you have no rights. You will come out right now without further discussion."

Immediately, the "battle" was over. The spirit left because I understood that Jesus had given me authority over all the power of the devil.

> I have given you authority to trample on snakes and scorpions and to overcome all the power of the enemy; nothing will harm you.
>
> — LUKE 10:19 NIV

The demon had to do what I told it to do. No excuses and no bargaining.

If you know the Word of God, *then you know the truth*. The Word of God gives us an indisputable foundation to stand on. We operate with the same authority Christ did when He walked the earth doing ministry.

BELIEVE THE WORD

The Word of God tells us what is possible for us, not our past experiences. The Word of God tells us who we are in God's eyes and explains clearly the authority we are given. Jesus Christ has given us authority over *all* the power of the enemy. The enemy has something that can be correctly called "power" but Jesus has given us authority over that power. He says that the enemy cannot harm us, and that we will "trample" the enemy.

Who does it sound like has the upper hand here? Do you believe the words of Jesus?

We don't have to earn anything. This authority is conferred upon us as sons and daughters of the King. When you are born again, you receive this authority as your birthright.

> Then Jesus came to them and said, "All authority in heaven and on earth has been given to me."
>
> — MATTHEW 28:18 NIV

The Father gave Jesus "all authority" and then Jesus delegated His authority to us. But remember, a prince who doesn't understand his role in the kingdom—and the authority he has—can easily be taken advantage of by a deceiver.

But because I *know* my authority, I *expect* things to obey when I speak. When I tell pain to go, I expect it to go. Why? Because my Father has given me authority over pain, sickness, and disease. When I cast out a demon, I expect it to go. Why? Because my Father has given me authority over demons.

This is not arrogance. This is simply faith in God. I believe what He says about me and my status as His son.

One time when I was about to pray for a man's injured leg, he told me, "It won't work."

I asked, "Why do you say that?"

"I know it won't work because I have had a hundred

people pray for me before you, and I still haven't been healed!"

In the natural, maybe I could have accepted this as a valid objection. After all, the natural mind says that if something has been tried a hundred times and it "didn't work" then there's probably no use in trying again. However, in that moment, I just recalled the authority I have been given. This enabled me to respond in faith.

"Well, it doesn't matter how many times you've been prayed for. I will command it and this time it's going to happen!"

He still wasn't buying it. He just shook his head, but I took up my authority and commanded his leg to be healed. To his surprise, the leg was instantly made whole!

If you don't know your authority, challenges can arise that can cause you to question your own rights to use that authority. If you question your own authority, your faith will not be very strong and the results you get might not be great. It's important to get settled on the issue of authority.

You have it.

The only thing that can keep you from walking in it is you!

YOU ARE GOD'S PLAN A AND HE HAS NO PLAN B

God created us knowing the whole time that man would fall. He also knew that He would have to pay the ultimate price to redeem man—His Son's life. But amazingly enough, He decided we were worth it!

In my mind's eye, I can almost see the Father saying to Himself, "I know it's going to happen. Man will fall and I will have to come down and save him, but it's worth it. It's worth any price because in the end, when My plan is finished, My house will be filled with sons and daughters and they will live with Me forever. I will pour My love out upon them and they will share their love with Me."

That is God's design—not man's. That is God's plan —not man's. He saved you and me when we were hopelessly lost in our sins, and He gave us His righteousness. He also adopted us as His children. He then gave us eternal life and prepared a place for us to live with Him forever, because that's what He wants. He wants to spend eternity with you and me.

Don't ask me to explain that kind of love, because the natural (carnal) mind cannot comprehend it. Instead, you will have to believe it in your spirit and accept it as fact because it is written in God's Word.

If you think your sins are too great for the Lord to forgive, then you are giving very little credit to the greatness of God's love. If your sins are greater than God's love, then obviously, you can't be forgiven. But if God's love is greater than your sins, then your forgiveness is assured.

His love for us is one way to prove our authority in Him. He gave no other creature or being the same affection He bestowed upon us humans—His children. His plan A.

THE THRONE OF GOD

Did you know that a throne is not just a chair? No, it's much more than just a chair. A throne is a symbol of power and authority. There is a throne in Heaven and everything must bow its knee before that throne. Here is the most interesting part about that throne as it relates to us: The Bible tells us that we are seated with Christ on His throne in heavenly places, and that we're seated there with Jesus at this very moment!

In Ephesians 2:6 (NIV) the Bible says, "And God raised us up with Christ and seated us with him in the heavenly realms in Christ Jesus."

Where is Jesus seated? He's seated on His throne. So if you are seated with Him, where are you seated? You are seated on His throne!

This truth was never more evident to me than it was when I met Cam Ward. See, Cam was a two-time world champion in mixed martial arts fighting in his early thirties. Can you imagine the injuries Cam's body must have endured as a professional punching bag? I can't. And I don't want to!

At the time, Cam had recently undergone surgery to relieve debilitating pain from his injured L5 disc, S1 nerve root, and back injuries. Damage to the L5 disc is particularly painful—not to mention dangerous —as it represents a transitional region from your lumbar spine to your lower back, and is responsible for helping to transfer the load from the spine to the pelvis. In other words, if your L5 is shot, your entire body is too.

And Cam's was shot. In fact, Cam described his pain as an 8.5—and this coming from someone who endured pain for a living! He couldn't even bend over and touch his toes. I didn't know the whole story at the time I prayed for him, but I learned later that his mother had followed me on YouTube and had flown her son in from out of state just to receive prayer that evening.

Cam had seen surgeons, physical therapists, and chiropractors, but none could provide the relief he needed to complete daily tasks without extreme discomfort.

When I prayed for Cam, I commanded the disc to be made new, and for all of the pain and restriction to go. Then I asked Cam to test things out. All of the pain was gone! Do you know why? Because my commandment came from the same position in Heaven as God the Father and Jesus. Because my commandment came from the highest throne that has been and will ever be.

Afterward, Cam tried to do what he had previously been unable to do. He twisted, he bent over, he touched his toes, and all movement and motion had been completely restored.

This kind of thing is a common occurrence for us, but Cam came to me at the end of the service to report that he hadn't been too sure about all the "healing stuff" his mother had been into. But now, he had no doubts whatsoever. That's the power of our positioning with Christ.

If you would like to see some of Cam's testimony, it can be found on my YouTube channel under the title: *World Champion MMA Fighter Cam Ward Healed by Jesus! –Tom Loud*

The throne in Heaven is a place of power. Since He is in us, and us in Him, we join Him on the throne beside God the Father, sharing in that power.

Every principality is under His feet and we are in His body. Every spiritual being that is not on the throne must bow to Him and to you (by extension of His authority in you). That includes angels, demons, principalities, and powers. Things in the physical realm and the spiritual realm must bow to you because you are seated with Christ in the position of ultimate authority.

Understanding your positioning with Jesus in the "heavenly realms" is critical to taking hold of the power offered to you through His Holy Spirit.

I HAVE, I GIVE

Let's take a look at what a healing prayer looks like when prayed from an understanding of our authority in Christ.

In Acts 3:1-8 (NIV) the Bible says, "One day Peter and John were going up to the temple at the time of prayer—at three in the afternoon. Now a man who was lame from birth was being carried to the temple gate called Beautiful, where he was put every day to beg from those going into the temple courts. When he saw Peter and John about to enter, he asked them for money. Peter looked straight at him, as did John. Then Peter said, 'Look at us!' So the man gave them his attention, expecting to get something from them. Then Peter said, 'Silver or gold I do not have, but what I do have I give you. In the name of Jesus Christ of Nazareth, walk.' Taking him by the right hand, he helped him up, and instantly the man's feet and ankles became strong. He jumped to his feet and began to walk. Then he went with them into the temple courts, walking and jumping, and praising God."

Peter knew his authority as a son of God. Peter did not ask the Father to heal the man. Peter took ownership of his responsibility to utilize the authority that God had given him. Peter said, "What I do have I give you. In the name of Jesus Christ of Nazareth, walk."

He was saying, "I have, I give." Then the man who was lame from birth was instantly healed and began to walk and leap for the first time in his life. Peter understood how to function in the authority that he had been given.

This ability is not specific to Peter only. Every other healing that was found in the book of Acts that occurred as a result of a disciple's prayers followed the same pattern. It's a pattern we can follow too.

One day when I was training a brother from our church, I took him to our local bus depot to look for people to minister to. We watched as a bus pulled up and dropped off a woman who was in a wheelchair.

We approached the woman to find out whether or not we could pray for her. After introducing ourselves, she said that her name was Maya. I asked Maya what was physically wrong with her. She recounted a severe accident she had been involved in where her car was broadsided by another vehicle, crushing her entire left side from neck to feet.

Maya was unable to walk and had pain from top to bottom. I told her that Jesus could heal her if she would let us pray.

She said, "Yes, please do."

I laid my hand on Maya's upper extremities and prayed, commanding every part of her body to be restored to the way it had been before the accident, and for all of the pain to leave immediately. One by one, every part of Maya's body was healed and all of the pain left.

Then, feeling rather bold, I said, "Would you like to try to walk?"

Maya said she was willing to give it a try. Moving aside the foot pads on her wheelchair, she braced herself and stood. And she walked!

Maya was completely healed and walked away pushing her wheelchair home. If you would like to see some of Maya's testimony, it can be found on my YouTube channel under the title: *"Get out of that wheelchair and walk!" Jesus heals years of pain.*

I have, I gave. You have, you can give too.

When some people hear me pray, they get offended and say things like, "Who do you think you are, commanding God what to do?" They really don't understand what's going on. I'm not commanding God. I am commanding everything that has been put under our authority, which includes sickness, demons, and even nature itself.

Jesus did these same things and then told us that we would do them. The problem is our unbelief in what the Word of God clearly says. If we aren't careful, we can have a greater trust and belief in our experiences, the experiences of others, and the traditions that have been taught by others than we do in the Word of God. Ask yourself if any of those things should be put above His authority. No! Read Psalm 138:2 (ESV):

I bow down toward your holy temple and give thanks to your name for your steadfast love and your faithfulness, for you have exalted above all things your name and your word.

Peter said that he had something. He said that what he had he was giving to the lame man, and that lame man received his healing. I have what Peter had and so do you. I received the Holy Spirit who possesses all the power of the kingdom and He desires to demonstrate that kingdom through me just like He did with Peter. And not just me, but every child of God. If the kingdom of God lives in you, then everything in the kingdom can come through you—if you allow it.

This is what Jesus told us to do with what He has given us.

Freely you have received; freely give.

— MATTHEW 28:18 NIV

You can argue with the Word, but it's far better to simply believe it.

DO I HAVE THE GIFT OF HEALING?

There are a few common questions that come up when we are speaking of walking in the gifts of the Spirit as opposed to walking in the authority of the believer. That might sound like an odd distinction, but we must understand that every person in the body of Christ is given certain gifts that they can operate in without much knowledge. However, the power of the Holy Spirit to perform the miraculous can be accessed by any believer as the occasion necessitates—as long as they understand their authority.

For example, the gift of healing. Some people say, "I don't know if I can heal because I don't have the gift of healing." I want you to know that if you are filled with the Holy Spirit, whether you have the gift of healing or not, you can heal because you have been given God's authority. That authority can be used against every work of the adversary, including sickness and infirmity.

We are seated with Christ in a much greater position of authority than His disciples had prior to the cross. Jesus was speaking to those pre-cross disciples in Luke 10:19. He said, "Look, I have given you authority over all the power of the enemy. You can walk among snakes and scorpions and crush them. Nothing will injure you" (My paraphrase).

Even before the Holy Spirit was sent to fill men's hearts, Jesus gave the disciples authority over the power of the enemy! "All" means anything that the enemy can do.

Seventy-two of these men were sent out by Jesus. They were amazed that nothing could withstand the commands spoken by them, which included healing and casting out evil spirits (Luke 10:17).

So, if a person doesn't need the gift of healing to be able to heal, then what is the point of having that gift? Think about that. It's a very valid question that deserves an answer. I have a theory on that.

Imagine that you see a person playing a complex Chopin composition on the piano. The person at the piano is 35 years old, and they've been practicing for 20 years. You could easily understand that because of the long and diligent practice they've put in, they've become very accomplished. Their accomplishment can be attributed to a lot of hard work.

Now, suppose you see a person playing the same Chopin composition that is only four years old and they're playing it flawlessly—perhaps even better than the person who has practiced for 20 years. The most experience that a four-year-old could boast would be one or two years. That would mean that they had accomplished that level of competency in an amazingly short period of time.

What would you say about a prodigy like that? Most would say, "They have a gift." Such a gift goes far beyond any natural level of learning. In fact, it could be called some kind of innate, almost superhuman ability that many would say was from God.

I have found that occasionally I discover some individuals who indeed have the gift of healing. Without any training and knowledge at all, they step right into it. They are praying for people and seeing miraculous healings that they simply can't explain. If you have been given the gift of healing, it will probably be something that you will discover by accident. One day you will pray for someone, they will be healed, and you will be as surprised as they are!

In these cases, God has given an individual a supernatural gifting that works as if it were a natural reflex that required no conscious effort or thought. It seems to come naturally to them. If, however, you don't have the gift of healing, you could pray the same way that the person with the gift prays, and yet you might get no results at all. That's where knowledge comes in.

With the proper knowledge, you can skillfully utilize the authority that God has given to His children and the same results can be accomplished.

I used to read books on how to heal the sick by some of the most famous healing ministers, and yet their methods didn't work for me. I believe that when certain people have success in healing miracles, they write books about how to perform them, but they do not understand that what comes naturally to them doesn't come naturally to the rest of us.

Because they are unaware of this fact, they say things like, "All you do is pray and have faith!" The problem is that they do not realize that those of us without the gift need to understand how to apply the correct principles—principles that these gifted people have never had to employ because they possess the gift.

For the rest of us, we will need to get the method straight before we can see the miraculous occur. We need to get a clear understanding of our authority and how to properly apply it to get the results we desire. We need to be trained before we can effectively use the powerful tools God has given to each of us.

Know that regardless of whether or not you have the gift, you can reach out to people and heal, deliver, and demonstrate the kingdom of God whenever you choose to.

YOUR AUTHORITY IS ENOUGH

Another common question regarding our gifting is: Does anyone have all the gifts of the Holy Spirit besides Jesus?

Well, I'll tell you that none of us has all of the gifts in their full proportion, but everyone has access to all of the gifts at any time they are required. This is possible because the Holy Spirit lives inside of you. The Holy Spirit, who lives within every born-again person, has all of the gifts of the Spirit with Him at all times.

There are times that I've been used in things that aren't my primary gifting. Healing is one example. Healing is not my primary gifting, but I can operate in healing through my authority as a son of God when it's necessary. I've been used in prophecy, words of knowledge, and working of miracles at various times. However, none of those are my primary area of gifting.

If someone needs healing, Jesus can be the healer. He can do that through you. You don't have to wait for someone to come along that has the gift because they are not always present where the need is. When the need is there, God through His Holy Spirit meets the need through anyone who is submitted to Him.

People will also ask me, "What about fasting?"

Some people think, "I'm going to need to get myself really holy and really sanctified and in this very special place before I can walk in authority on these things, so I better start fasting."

There is, of course, nothing wrong with fasting, praying, or sanctifying your life to the Lord. But that doesn't buy you any more power than you were given at the new birth.

Some like to point at things like that time Jesus' disciples tried to cast an unclean spirit out of a young boy and they couldn't do it. Then the father of the young boy brought his child to Jesus and said, "I took him to your disciples, but they couldn't cast the spirit out."

And Jesus said, "Well, it's because of their (your) little faith. But this kind comes not out, but by prayer and fasting" (Matthew 17:19-21, my paraphrase).

Now, you might think that this demon is of a particular type that you've got to really fast, pray, and get yourself all straightened out before you will be powerful enough to cast out. More fasting would not have gotten them more authority, but it was prescribed to these disciples to address the root problem—their flesh.

Jesus was saying that the apostles' flesh was getting in the way. They were not being spiritually minded, but they were operating from the carnal mind, the mind of the flesh.

Fasting is not for the purpose of weakening an evil spirit, because it doesn't do that. Rather, fasting is a way to get our flesh under subjection to the Holy Spirit. Once you get your flesh out of the way by weakening it a bit, your spirit moves without further hindrance. That's all it does. It doesn't make you a more powerful person. It just makes the flesh a less powerful influence.

THE SOURCE OF ALL AUTHORITY

Jesus demonstrates to us how the Son of God applies His authority when it is required to accomplish God's will. In Mark 11:27-28, the scribes and the Pharisees approached Jesus as He was going through their town. He was behaving as if He had authority. And, of course, He did. These men didn't understand how Jesus possessed this kind of authority, so they asked Him, "Who gave you this authority? By what authority do you do these things?"

That's something that is important for us to answer. We need to know by what authority we do these things. For example, when healing the sick, by what authority are you doing it? We must recognize how authority works—that someone with a higher level of authority has the right to give or delegate that authority to anyone they choose, and Jesus has chosen you and me.

There have been times when I have been doing marketplace ministry and I have had the opportunity to lead the lost to the Lord. Sometimes, these are people who have previously had no knowledge of God and knew very little about the supernatural. After leading some of these people to Jesus, I have taken the person, who is only minutes old in the faith, and instructed them on how to pray for their friend standing right next to them.

Time and time again, these people who knew almost nothing have prayed for their companion and witnessed a miracle through their own hands. I know how it works, even though they don't. But by simply doing as I instructed, the miracle manifested for them immediately.

Let me give you an example. I was invited to come to the Detroit, Michigan, area to teach marketplace ministry to a church that wanted to begin walking in the miraculous. I taught the first meeting on a Friday night, and the next day I was going to take groups out into public to pray for people.

At the end of the meeting, I thought that I was going to my hotel room, but the pastor had another idea.

Before I could dismiss everyone, a church leader came up to the front and asked, "Who in here needs healing? We are looking for the impossible case so that Tom can demonstrate to us what he just taught."

No pressure there! In the back of the room was a gentleman who raised his hand and said that he was certainly the worst case in the building. His name was Will, and all eyes were on me to perform the fantastic miracle. I really felt on the spot. Within my heart I said, "Lord, you've got to come through for me here!"

Will enumerated a long list of medical problems having to do with his heart, respiration, mobility, etc. Then Will told us that he could not walk more than ten feet without becoming completely exhausted and out of breath. Then I found out one other interesting thing about Will—he thought that healing was not for today. Will's boss had dragged him to the meeting after work and Will wasn't really interested in going.

I had a huge challenge in front of me, but I couldn't back out. I prayed for Will, commanding complete healing for his heart, his lungs, and everything else that was wrong with his body.

There was no lightning from heaven, no dramatic display. In fact, nothing on the outside appeared any different. All eyes were watching.

Everyone was wondering, *"Had God healed Will?"*

I told Will to walk around the church. He walked 10 feet, then 20, then 30 . . . no signs of exhaustion. I then said, "Run up and down the front steps of the church." And he did. Then Will decided he would walk around the whole city block where the church was located.

All of Will's pain had vanished, his fatigue was gone, and his energy was restored.

The next day I personally took Will with me to do marketplace ministry. Will walked miles with me, and not only was he without any signs of fatigue, but he also was praying for people and seeing miracles at his own hand! Will—the man who hours earlier had confessed his belief that healings were not for today's Christian.

FAITH THROUGH THE FAITHLESS

Here is something else that will come as a great challenge for some to believe, just as it was for me when I first witnessed it: There have been times when I have chosen a person who was not yet a believer to operate in healing. I have instructed them to pray for their unsaved friend and the healing miracle occurred without them knowing Jesus as their Savior.

I know that sounds impossible, but some things are only impossible because we don't have the faith to believe for them. The reason that I can instruct an unbeliever to pray for their friend and then see a miracle is because of delegated authority. This is possible when someone who actually has authority directs someone else to carry out an action by following the orders of the one who legitimately has the authority.

A president can order a corporal in the army to arrest a man of higher rank, such as a colonel. It is not the superiority of the corporal's authority that makes this possible, but the authority of the president who is giving the command. In the same way, I can ask somebody to do something under my authority—just as Jesus did—and the miracle will occur.

Do you remember when the disciples were fishing and Jesus appeared and asked them how they were doing? Let's look at John 21:4-6 (NIV). It says: "Early in the morning, Jesus stood on the shore, but the disciples did not realize that it was Jesus. He called out to them, 'Friends, haven't you any fish?' 'No,' they answered. He said, 'Throw your net on the right side of the boat and you will find some.' When they did, they were unable to haul the net in because of the large number of fish."

The disciples didn't have faith for what was about to happen, but they carried out the instructions of Jesus, who had the authority. And the miracle occurred.

Where do I get my authority? From Jesus, of course! When I pray for the sick, I am simply following the instructions that Jesus gave me, so the miracle manifests. What am I talking about? When did Jesus tell me to pray for the sick?

In Matthew 10:7-8 (BSB) the Bible says, "As you go, preach this message: 'The kingdom of heaven is near.' Heal the sick, raise the dead, cleanse the lepers, drive out demons. Freely you have received; freely give."

Don't ever let anyone talk you into believing that the miracles of God—the same miracles that manifested at the hands of Jesus' early followers— have passed away. Also, never get stuck in the trap of believing that this power was only for the 12 apostles, because that simply is not true. That power is available to all who believe.

In Mark 16:16-17 (BSB) the Bible says: "Whoever believes and is baptized will be saved, but whoever does not believe will be condemned. And these signs will accompany those who believe: In My name, they will drive out demons; they will speak in new tongues; they will pick up snakes with their hands, and if they drink any deadly poison, it will not harm them; they will lay their hands on the sick, and they will be made well."

Who was this passage written about? "Whoever believes." Where do Todd White, Pete Cabrera Jr., or Tom Loud get their authority?" From Jesus. Jesus gave us all the same authority. When He said all His believers can lay their hands on the sick and the sick will recover, that's what He meant.

I live in the Seattle area, and in the summer, I like to go to the "Seattle Center" and do marketplace ministry. This is the location where the 1962 World's Fair was held, and where the famous Space Needle still stands today. I like to look for challenges to stretch my faith and force myself to get out of my comfort zone—to grow my own faith.

One beautiful August day I saw a group of young people out on the lawn in front of the great fountain practicing for their ballet performance. I walked right into the middle of about eight young people and introduced myself. I asked if any of them had any pain because Jesus would like to heal them.

I had a number of young people come forward and see the power of God and many were healed. One in particular was a young woman named Haley. This is a different Haley from the one that was my first miraculous healing. "Haley Two" was a case of particular interest because she had absolutely no faith in God—God's healing power had never even entered her mind!

Haley had been born with severe scoliosis of the spine. In fact, she could not even stretch her right arm diagonally across her body. The scoliosis caused pain and restriction in movement—especially troubling for a young ballerina and aspiring professional dancer. Up until that point, doctors had been unable to offer Haley any hope at all.

I asked Haley to demonstrate the restriction until it hurt. She did, reporting that the movement caused a pain level of nine. I didn't even touch Haley—I just held my hand over her back and commanded the scoliosis to go. That's right—I demonstrated the authority I had in the son of God by using a *shadow* to pray a miraculous healing over Haley's back.

I prayed, commanding the back, muscles, tendons, ligaments, and vertebrae to be healed. After a moment or two, I told Haley to do what she could not do before.

Haley then stretched her right arm diagonally across her chest all the way to the other side of her torso without any restriction at all. "It's like a zero!" she said of her pain level. The look of surprise on her face was priceless. This was the first time in her life she was able to move normally!

Haley grinned from ear to ear and said, "The doctors were never able to do this!"

Then I told Haley that Jesus had healed her because He loved her, and I asked her if she would like to receive Him as her Savior. She said, "Yes," and I led her and two of her friends in a salvation prayer that very day.

If you would like to see some of Haley's testimony, it can be found on my YouTube channel under the title: *Youth Ballet Troop Healed, Saved, Blown Away!!! – Tom Loud*

So, all of the disciples of Jesus (that's you and me) have been told to go and heal the sick and injured. The authority we have through Him is so great that we can even use a shadow to transfer its power. Because He has given us this command, He has delegated His authority to us.

It's absolutely true! You and I can all do these things because we all have been given authority by Jesus, who is the highest authority of all.

Very truly I tell you, whoever believes in me will do the works I have been doing, and they will do even greater things than these, because I am going to the Father.

— JOHN 14:12 NIV

5

THE KEY OF OVERCOMING THE CARNAL MIND

You're probably wondering how and when you'll be able to make the switch from carnal thinking to spiritual, demonstrating God's power—the power you've been so abundantly given through His Holy Spirit. That is coming up very soon, but first I want to share a few stories that may help give you context to the process.

Todd White is an evangelist that you may have heard of. He has had a very impactful ministry involving the demonstration of healing miracles and words of knowledge. Though many people have been healed and saved through his ministry, Todd prayed for something like 500 people before he saw his first healing! I could have never persisted that long. If I prayed for 10 people and saw no results, I would have concluded that I just did not have what it took to pray for someone's healing.

Then there's my friend Pete Cabrera Jr. Pete was

inspired by the videos Todd had posted about his ministry, and Pete began praying for miraculous healings just like he saw Todd doing. Much like with Todd's testimony, Pete prayed for around 300 people before he saw his first miracle. Again, I would have never lasted that long.

In fact, Pete got so frustrated in his pursuit of praying miraculous healings that he issued a challenge to God. He said, "Lord, I'm going to pray for somebody just like Todd did, and if there isn't a healing, I'm done!"

The next day Pete encountered a man with a back problem. Just as he'd seen Todd do, he approached the man and asked if he could pray for him. In his mind, Pete reminded himself that this prayer was his last-ditch effort to see if anything would happen. Pete figured nothing was going to happen.

When the man agreed to let Pete pray for him, Pete didn't put much heart or effort into it. In fact, he wrote Todd's prayer on his hand and just read it over the man. When he was finished, Pete asked the man to test out his back.

With a bewildered look on his face, the man said, "The pain is gone!"

But do you know what happened next? Pete didn't believe him!

Pete said, "Come on, man. Don't play with me. I'm serious about this!"

The man said, "No, really. I'm not kidding. The pain is gone!" He had been healed of his back pain.

This was the breakthrough Pete needed. Since that day, thousands have been healed through Pete's prayers, and tens of thousands through Pete's students.

THE DAY I LEARNED NOTHING

My story of miraculous healings is entangled with Pete's, as he is the one who unknowingly showed me how to take hold of the key to the spirit mind.

One day I was in my office and my secretary asked me to look at a video that she had stumbled upon while searching the internet. In this video, I saw a man I had never heard of named Pete Cabrera Jr. This man was doing something that appeared really wild, and outside of the realm of anything I had ever witnessed before.

Pete ran a soup kitchen at the time, and many people came in with a variety of physical problems. One day a man and his wife came into Pete's office and the man was complaining of a severe back problem. Pete had the man sit down in a chair and put up his feet on a coffee table. Then Pete handed the camera to this man's wife (who, by the way, was an atheist) and asked her to video what he was about to do.

Pete instructed the man to sit up straight in his chair and extend his legs out until they were sitting on top of the coffee table. This couple had only just met Pete and had no idea what he was about to do.

As the man rested his legs in a fully extended position on the table, it was obvious that one was significantly shorter than the other. Pete then pointed to the shorter of the two legs and said, "Come out, come even!"

Without a moment's hesitation, the shorter leg grew out to match the other one! I was surprised, but the atheist wife that was filming was shocked to her core.

A growing leg would have been enough for me to wonder if it were real or a hoax, but then things got even weirder! Pete pointed at the leg that was originally longer and commanded it, "Come out! More, more, more." To my amazement, the leg grew out about three inches!

Then Pete told the man to stand up and walk. Having one leg three inches longer than the other, the man had a difficult time. At this point, the wife was completely freaking out and so was her husband. Pete had the man sit down again and alternately grew and shrunk back both legs, apparently at will.

When the whole exercise had come to an end, the man's back pain was gone. The wife wasn't so sure about her atheism anymore. The man was completely healed and I was completely dumbfounded. I questioned what I saw. I wondered, "Could this be real or just a clever fraud? Who is this Pete guy? Is he legitimate or a fake?"

I began researching Pete Cabrera Jr., and at the time, he was relatively unknown. There was very little information about him available. I decided I would watch the video in slow motion, frame by frame, to see if I could detect any tampering or deceptive editing. I found none. I then began to watch other videos of his, and I eventually determined that he was genuine and the people he was praying for were not actors.

I had to find out how he was accomplishing these miraculous healings, many of which outshined anything I had ever seen, even at the hands of the world's most famous "faith healers." In these simple, unedited videos, people were being healed of every kind of sickness and infirmity that you could name. Sometimes, Pete would heal with a spoken word, and other times, he would heal with no words at all. Sometimes, he would touch them, and at other times, he wouldn't touch them.

But regardless of what he did, it seemed that people were getting legitimately and dramatically healed. I wanted to know what his secret was, because I had been praying for people for a very long time and had not experienced that kind of success. I could find no listed number or email for Pete, so I tried to contact him by sending messages to him through his YouTube channel.

I waited, waited, and heard nothing. Then one day months later, out of the blue (and long after I had given up hope for a response), I got a phone call from Pete at my office. I answered the phone and he said, "Hi, is this Tom Loud? This is Pete Cabrera Jr. I'm at Walmart right now buying some milk. What can I do for you?"

I said, "Wow, I'm really honored that you called me, Mr. Cabrera. I have a question for you."

He said, "Shoot."

The video I asked Pete about was one where he prayed for a woman's shoulder. In the video, Pete prayed a simple prayer for her: "Father, I thank you for this woman. In Jesus' name, I speak to this shoulder and rotator cuff and I tell it to become whole."

The woman lifted her arm out to the side. While she had more movement than she had before the prayer, it was still not operating in full range.

Pete said, "Let me pray again." He took hold of her hand and then touched her shoulder. Then, Pete just looked at her shoulder. He stood there not doing anything else for several seconds before saying, "Try it again."

This time, the lady was able to hold her hand high in the air—she had complete mobility. But, wait. What had happened the second time he prayed? Had he actually been praying at all?

When I got Pete on the phone I said, "I've got to know. At the times you're not saying anything during your healing prayers, what is it that you're doing? Are you imagining the healing as a done work? Are you praying silently in your head and heart? I want to know what's going through your mind at those moments."

Here is what Pete said back to me: "Tom, I was thinking nothing."

"Nothing? You were thinking nothing?"

"I wasn't thinking or praying anything."

I said, "Is that your answer? Is that it?"

He replied, "That's it. That's my answer. I was thinking nothing."

I was more than a little bit let down. It was like the air in my balloon had suddenly leaked out and I was completely deflated. He gave me nothing to take hold of. His answer was basically no answer at all. None of it made any sense.

I felt like one of the androids in the Star Trek episode where Captain Kirk said, "I always lie."

That statement is impossible to understand using logic. If you say, "I always lie," then that, too, must be a lie, meaning you always tell the truth. But if you always tell the truth, how can you say you always lie?

At that point, the evil android's brains were fried, and as they began to smoke from their ears, they said, "Does not compute! Does not compute!"

What Pete had said did not compute. He was praying and then the healing occurred, but he was saying nothing, thinking nothing, and feeling nothing!

In a fit of great frustration, I prayed to the Lord and said, "Jesus, what does that mean?" I was determined to find the answer to that question, whatever it took. I mean, how can you be praying for somebody and not even be thinking about it? That made no sense at all to me.

And it wouldn't until much later.

There's something else I want you to know about Pete Cabrera Jr. Pete spent two years studying an extensive course in healing taught by Curry Blake. It's called Divine Healing Technician Training, or DHT. He also prayed for many people, but still never saw healing and couldn't figure out why. After studying DHT and then stumbling upon Todd White's videos, Pete stepped out to pray for people to be healed, but after having no

TOM LOUD

success, he began to get frustrated and was about ready to quit.

Just before throwing in the towel, Pete watched *one* more Todd White video, and he noticed how Todd prayed so simply and effortlessly, and as a result, people received their healing. Pete began to get a little upset. In his heart he said, "It can't be that easy! I've been stepping out in faith and praying my guts out. This guy just walks up to somebody and says, 'Hey dude! Want to see something crazy? Watch this!', and the person is healed!"

But I have good news for you—you don't need to wait as long as Todd and Pete did to experience the miraculous. You can start seeing miracles the first time you step out and pray. It's all about having the correct keys.

THE BEAUTY OF NOTHING

I saw what Pete was doing, but I didn't know exactly how his process worked. I heard his words and I saw the results, but there was something that I couldn't see. I couldn't see what was going on inside of Pete's head or heart, and I was convinced that the answer to that question was the key that I was missing.

Before I let Pete off the phone, I asked another question. I said, "In the shoulder video, how did you know how long to wait before telling her to try it again?"

Pete said, "I don't know. I just gave the Lord time to work."

I got off the phone with Pete feeling as if I'd just learned nothing new. But then the Lord brought Romans 8:7 to mind.

> Because the carnal mind *is* enmity against God; for it
> is not subject to the law of God, nor indeed can be.
>
> — ROMANS 8:7 NKJV

The word "carnal" here is the Greek word *sarkos*, which simply means "flesh." The carnal mind (natural, fleshly mind) is enmity against God. The word "enmity" used here is the Greek word *echthra*, which means "hostile." So your natural, fleshly "carnal mind" is not only incapable of understanding or receiving the things of the Spirit, but it is actually hostile towards God and unable to accept or believe God's Word.

You might say, "Hostile? That's an aggressive word. I don't think my natural mind feels hostile toward God." Let me explain.

In school I found myself saying, "I hate math," in a completely hostile way. But why would I be hostile towards math? I was hostile towards math because when I got to a certain level, it frustrated me that I was not good at math. Someone began mixing the alphabet with numbers, and suddenly, I found myself frustrated in the attempt to understand the lunacy.

I got frustrated trying to understand that which did

not make clear sense and this frustration made me angry. I said, "I am trying my best to understand this, but I just don't get it!"

That's what happens with the carnal mind when God says, "Believe this," and the carnal mind says, "But how is that possible? I just can't accept that." If it doesn't make sense, the carnal mind will not receive it. But you have to understand that the mind of Christ in you speaks differently.

It says, "I don't need to think about it. If God has spoken it, it's simply fact."

Romans 8:7 teaches us that the natural, carnal mind is "not subject to the laws of God, neither can be."

So, what exactly does this tell us about the attributes and limitations of the natural, fleshly, and carnal mind? It tells us that it is not subject to God's laws. The word "subject" here is the Greek word *hupotassó*, meaning to submit and to put into subjection. In other words, the natural, fleshly, carnal mind is not submitted to God's Word.

You may have been told that in order to overcome your mind's natural hostility toward God, you must renew your mind. The problem is many people have defined the method of renewing the mind incorrectly. I did it for many years also. I had been taught that renewing the mind was a process of reprogramming the old mind—the carnal mind. I was taught that it was a process of filling the mind with so much of the Word of God that it finally comes into subjection and under the control of God. I had believed that someday, if I just tried long enough and hard enough, my mind would come into a state of faith and in full agreement with the Word of God. However, Romans 8:7 tells us that this is simply not possible.

Your carnal (natural) mind will never agree with the Word of God because it is incapable of doing so. Back in those days, I read the Word, meditated on the Word, and repeatedly declared the Word aloud. I practiced positively confessing what it said for over thirty years in the hope that faith would just all of a sudden fill my heart, and I would have no more doubt. But that never happened.

It was a good and profitable exercise, but it never removed doubt from my mind when I prayed. I would pray in faith and that little voice in the background would always be there saying, "But what if it doesn't work? What if you don't have enough faith?" Instead of thinking of the process of renewing your mind as a process of fixing up your old, carnal, and natural mind, begin to think of it as renewing the method of how you process information.

We must begin to retrain ourselves in the way we do our thinking. When we are operating in the realm of the physical world, we engage our natural (carnal) mind, but when we are operating in the realm of spiritual things, we disengage our natural mind and utilize the mind of the spirit. We must begin to operate in this new way and establish new habits.

Our carnal mind *can only believe* what it can see. It cannot understand the spiritual realm, nor discern what the Spirit of God wants or desires. Instead of praying and then waiting to see what would happen, worrying and begging God to move, I learned to lay my hands on people and say, "In the name of Jesus, be made whole." Then, to pause and think nothing.

During this time, I'm quieting my carnal mind. There are those voices that want to say, "What if this doesn't work?" I tell them to be quiet and sit in the corner. I don't need my carnal mind's help. I'm busy working in the spiritual realm.

See, we have been given the mind of Christ. And it's with this mind that we need to operate from when praying a prayer of healing for someone. We need to understand scriptures using that mind. Move in the spirit without worrying about what we're thinking. What you're thinking is of no importance to you. Say what God would have you to say, then leave the rest to God and watch Him work. Take the carnal mind completely out of the equation. Disengage it. It cannot help you.

This is what Jesus meant when He said, "the flesh profits nothing." It cannot help you. It can only get in the way. So shut it off.

When the Lord gave me the answer I was looking for, I went out that very same day and prayed for people and saw miraculous healings immediately. I did not need to pray for a thousand or even a hundred people. That one revelation gave me all I needed to open the vault to God's miraculous power.

Since that day, I've seen thousands of healings on an ongoing basis, and I have had the privilege of training countless Christians just like you, who have never previously seen a firsthand miracle, to immediately see miracles occur at their own hands!

All I had needed for the miraculous to manifest was to change a thought. The whole time I was searching, that's all I had to do. I didn't have to get any supernatural visitation from Heaven—no special anointing. I didn't need to have a prophet with the gifts of healing lay hands on me. All I had to do was change my perspective, my way of thinking, and my way of seeing things.

You pray and then . . . think nothing.

Everything began to change for me once I understood the difference between operating from the carnal, natural mind, and instead operating from the mind of the spirit. All of our doubts, our fears, and our unbelief reside in our natural, carnal mind.

If you are like me, you thought that with enough study and discipline, you could take that natural mind and change it into something more spiritual. You can try, but what you are attempting to do is utterly impossible.

But fortunately, that's not the end of the story. In the same way I learned from Pete Cabrera, we have to go forward with the mind of the Spirit. Not just in prayers for healing, but in all operations involving the Holy Spirit.

You may ask yourself, "Do we really have access to a mind that is without doubt and unbelief? Is that really possible?" 1 Corinthians 2:16 (NIV) says: "Who has known the mind of the Lord so as to instruct

Him?" We don't tell God what He's capable of—He tells us.

PUT YOUR CARNAL MIND IN THE CORNER

It is essential to learn to put the carnal mind out of the room when you begin to operate in faith. If you are not diligent to do this, it will attempt to rise up and interfere, hindering the results you receive when you pray.

We cannot pray in faith if both minds are engaged. That's what the Bible means when it tells us not to be "double-minded." Here is what being "double-minded" will produce in prayer:

> But he must ask in faith, without doubting, because he who doubts is like a wave of the sea, blown and tossed by the wind. The man should not expect to receive anything from the Lord. He is a double-minded man, unstable in all his ways.
>
> — JAMES 1:6-7 NIV

God's Word says that if you lack something, you can ask God and He will give it freely. But a double-minded man wavers between the faith that is in his spiritual mind and the doubt that is in his carnal mind. Remember, the carnal mind does not have faith. It only has doubt, so it has to be disengaged. When you start trying to figure out how God is going to do something, or how something could possibly happen by faith, then you are engaging your carnal mind. You've become double-minded. This creates a condition of instability where it becomes impossible to truly stand in unwavering faith without doubting. What this Scripture also clearly demonstrates is that it is indeed possible to be double-minded and you can't be double-minded unless you have two minds.

A double-minded man is a man that tries to have faith in God's Word while engaging his natural and carnal mind in the process. It cannot work. Faith and the carnal mind do not mix together successfully. These verses tell us that a double-minded man is unstable in all his ways—all of them.

So, we have to learn how to operate out of the right mind, the mind of the Spirit. We have to learn to put the carnal mind in its place, and keep it out of the way of our spiritual endeavors. We have to learn when it is appropriate to operate out of the carnal mind, and when we should be operating out of the mind of the Spirit.

The mind of Christ does not have the capacity to doubt His father. In the same way, there is no room for uncertainty when you are operating in the gifts of the Holy Spirit. Bringing your carnality under control is the only way to move toward single-mindedness, and by extension, toward effective prayers of healing. You do this by pushing those thoughts to the edge of your mind. Ignoring them. Telling them to go away, and leaving your mind clear for God to speak and work.

When I grasped this, I put it to the test on Haley (Haley One), who I have mentioned before as the first person that I prayed for and saw a miraculous healing. I used my authority to tell Haley's arthritis and pain to go, and then I paused and stilled myself. I "rested" in the Lord and did not allow my mind to speak at all. After a few moments, I asked her to test things out. She was completely healed!

One of the principles that will be key to moving in the realm of the miraculous is to remember that we have two minds. We have a "spiritual mind" and a "natural mind." Only those who have been born-again of the Spirit have their "spiritual mind" available for access. Those who have not been born-again of the Spirit have only the earthbound, natural, physical, and rational mind as their source.

BRINGING YOUR CARNAL MIND INTO SUBJECTION

When we can begin to recognize that our carnal mind is the one that has been sitting on the throne for most of our life—and that it is the one that has led us in many directions that have nothing to do with the Spirit—then we can understand where the problem lies in our attempts to walk out a Spirit-led life.

The truth is that many of our problems have their root in our carnal mind, which has not been put under subjection to the Holy Spirit. We must begin to learn how to discern which thoughts are of God and which thoughts are of the carnal mind, and then order our steps accordingly. This is what the Bible means when it tells you to take captive every thought to the obedience of Christ.

> We demolish arguments and every pretension that sets itself up against the knowledge of God, and we take captive every thought to make it obedient to Christ.

> — 2 CORINTHIANS 10:5 NIV

Taking something captive doesn't imply a negotiation. There's no discussion. We don't go back and forth reasoning with the carnal mind to get it to agree with God. As soon as we detect a thought from the carnal mind, we take it captive. We put it under subjection.

So, dear reader, I'm going to do my best to show you how to discern when the carnal mind is speaking and when the mind of Christ in you is speaking. When you learn the difference, you can put Christ on the throne of your heart and you can listen to the thoughts of the Spirit. Then you will be able to do the right things at the right time, unlocking the doors of God's kingdom to you.

Let me give you an example of a day when my carnal mind was on the throne and I almost robbed myself, the Lord, and an individual in need, of a miracle.

One day I wasn't in a good mood at all. I didn't really feel like praying for anyone. In my carnal mind, I said, "I don't want to go out ministering today. I'm tired and irritable. God probably couldn't work through my bad attitude anyway."

As soon as this thought entered my mind, my spirit rejected it. That thought was filled with doubt and fear —neither of which are from the Lord. I decided to use the situation to prove a powerful point. The point was this: Being a son of God is who we are when we feel spiritual *and* when we don't. And the miraculous is always possible simply because children of God carry authority. Being a child of God is a fact, whether you fasted that day or not. Whether you felt the presence of the Holy Spirit or not. Feelings have little to do with the facts when it comes to being spirit-minded.

I took out my GoPro camera, looked into the lens, and said, "I am really not feeling very spiritual right now, but I am going to do what I was made to do anyway. I was made to do the works of Him who called me out of darkness and into the light, on my good days *and* my bad days."

I proceeded to drive to the local bus depot. I was looking for my first opportunity like a lion looks for a limping gazelle. Yes, my attitude was poor, but I still carried the power and authority of a child of God.

Then I saw a man with a leg cast. I approached him and introduced myself and asked him what happened. His name was Duane. Duane had been a pedestrian in a crosswalk and he was hit by a car. I asked Duane if he had any pain, and he began to tell me of every spot on his body that had been injured. The list was quite long.

His foot had been broken in a dozen places, his leg had been smashed, his left arm had been broken so badly that it was put back together with screws and rods, his back was in great pain, and he didn't look much happier than I did that day.

I told Duane that if he let me pray for him, God would heal everything. He looked at me out of the corner of his eye with that look of sizing a person up, trying to determine if they are crazy or not. I wasn't terribly subtle, telling him that he had nothing to lose. He allowed me to pray.

I asked his pain level on a scale from one through 10 for each injury and then I spoke healing over them one by one. I prayed for his arm—it could not freely move in every direction and it was in great pain. I spoke a few words over it and he tolerated me with a scowl on his face.

Then I said, "Now test it out. Look for the pain." He scoffingly began to go through the motions, and then his countenance changed. It was as if a wave of surprise went over his face and suddenly, he was lit up with excitement.

He exclaimed, "It's gone . . . I feel no pain!" He was so excited that he could hardly wait for me to move on to the foot, the leg, the back, and a few other places. One by one each area was healed.

I asked him if he would like to take his leg cast off and see if he could walk without pain. He did, and he was completely healed. He went from having a scowl on his face to smiling from ear to ear.

If you would like to see some of the video of this encounter, it can be found on my YouTube channel under the title: *Hit by Car - Healed by Jesus!!!!*

If I had not practiced bringing my carnal mind under the Spirit's subjection, I may have believed its lies—that I could not heal anyone because of my own foul mood. But once the Spirit revealed Himself to my spirit mind, moving me to action, God showed how very little *I* have to do with *His* healing power.

MY FIRST EXPERIENCE THINKING NOTHING

Some of my problem came from the teachings of certain faith preachers that I listened to during the 1970s. There was a teaching that was prevalent back then, and it was based on Romans 12:2 (NKJV): "And do not be conformed to this world, but be transformed by the renewing of your mind, that you may prove what is that good and acceptable and perfect will of God."

The Word of God is always true, but sometimes the interpretation of what the Word says can be misconstrued. The teaching from this verse concerning "renewing the mind" became a staple of the faith movement in the 70s. The practical application of this verse went something like this: If a person would read God's Word, and then speak, or declare it aloud with their mouth repeatedly, eventually, the Word would "drop down into your spirit" and suddenly become unshakeable faith. Well, that sounded like a reasonable concept, so I did it, as you know, for over 30 years!

I prayed out powerfully with faith-filled words and declared healing over people, just like I do now, but nothing happened back then. Not only did nothing happen, but that voice was still speaking in my head, loud and clear, "What if it doesn't work? I will feel like a fool. I sure hope something will happen!"

Renewing the mind is indeed a biblical principle, but I no longer see the method that those preachers taught as a valid application of that verse. It really has nothing to do with a process of making your carnal mind line up with the Word of God.

All that I have explained in this book so far—about turning off the carnal mind and operating out of my spirit mind instead—came to me in an instant. Along with this revelation came an understanding about how this concept applies to praying for the miraculous. At the moment I received the revelation, I understood what I needed to do. At that point, it was still in the realm of theory, but it was an exciting theory. Before I could tell others about it, I would need to test it for myself.

I needed to see if Pete's answer of, "I wasn't thinking anything and I wasn't feeling anything," was going to make sense. What was communicated to me by the Holy Spirit was that the natural (carnal) mind needed to be set aside (disengaged) when it came to the act of praying in faith and without doubt.

I saw that what Pete was doing, and without even being aware of it, was shutting off his natural mind, thus removing it from the act of praying. When he said he "wasn't thinking anything," he was actually disengaging from any thought process for that moment.

But how does one do that? How do you stop your mind from thinking? Well, it was time to find out. It was time to see if I could actually pray without allowing my natural mind to get in the way.

Up to this point, I had never approached a stranger in public and asked if I could pray for them to experience a miraculous healing. I was determined to give it a try because I had a new perspective on the matter. I got up from my desk, climbed into my car, and drove off looking for my first candidate. I decide to stop at a strip mall and see if I could find someone that was in need of prayer.

Finally, I saw my chance. It was a young woman about 30 years old coming out of a Dollar Tree and she was using a walker. As it turned out, this was Haley (Haley One), who I mentioned a couple of times previously as my first healing miracle. I want to give more detail now so that you can get a full, practical picture of how God moved to put this principle into practice in my life.

I could see that Haley was having great difficulty walking, so I approached her and said, "Hi, my name is Tom. I pray for people and God heals them. Are you in any pain?"

Now, actually I had never prayed for anyone this way before, but it seemed like the words jumped out of my mouth before I had the chance to stop them.

The young woman told me her name, and that she had been crippled with osteoarthritis, fibromyalgia, and constant pain that doctors were unable to cure. She also had a large lump on the back of her neck that had been there for a long time. I asked her what her pain level was on a scale from one to 10. She said she was an eight. Then I asked her if she had any restriction of movement. I found out that she could only bend forward far enough to touch her knees, and that was only with great pain. Then I found myself asking her if I could pray for God to heal her right then and there and she said, "Yes."

This was it. This was my big chance. It was a big plus in my mind that she was a stranger because that meant if it didn't work, no one else would know. I put my hand on her and told her to just relax and let me pray. I prayed like this: "Heavenly Father, I thank You for Haley. I know that You love her and You don't want her to be in any pain. Right now, I speak to this arthritis. I command you to leave Haley's body now! Every muscle, tendon, ligament, and nerve, be healed now! Now, I speak to the pain. All pain leave, now!"

Then came the most critical part of the test. Immediately after finishing the prayer, I stopped all thought and simply rested and let God work while I kept my hand on her for a few moments. When my natural mind would begin to say things like, "What if it doesn't work?" I would tell it to shut up before the full thought could be formed. I paused, I rested, I hushed all thought, suspended all of my senses, and simply rested. After a few moments of not thinking, and of holding back my thoughts whenever they tried to engage, I took my hands off, looked at her, and said, "Touch your toes."

She looked at me as if I were crazy and said, "I can't do that!"

I heard myself saying, "You can now!"

She could tell that I was serious, so against every instinct, she bent forward all the way to her toes and then stood up and said, "It's gone! All of the pain is gone!"

I was shocked but excited. I said, "Please, be honest. Give it a test and look for the pain."

She could find none. She could move like she hadn't moved in years and the lump that was on her neck went away too! I had that *aha* moment like the man who just discovered the cure to a rare disease or like the man who solved the mystery that revealed the location of a vast, buried treasure.

I said to myself, "If this works for me, perhaps this is the breakthrough piece of knowledge that will cause many others to be able to see miracles at their hands also."

I got a call from Haley three months later. She was still completely free from all of the pain and infirmity that she had when I first met her, but she wanted to tell me that she had now been in an accident and wondered if I could pray for her again.

She was my first dramatic healing miracle, so of course I was glad to pray for her again. I arranged to meet her immediately. She informed me that she had broken her collarbone on the right side. She could not move her arm much and could not raise it above the height of her shoulder.

I prayed for her in the same manner I did the first time. She started to say, "That's weird. As you were praying, I felt things reattaching inside my chest and shoulder and all of the pain left."

I had her raise her arm and it went right over her head without any problem and without any pain!

Since that first day when I tested the theory out for myself, I have seen the Lord heal thousands of times, using this very same method. I am not simply saying that I discovered something that worked just for me, but in fact, I have taught this same principle to people around the world, and it has worked for people everywhere. It has even succeeded in places where the miraculous works of God had never been seen before.

Silencing the mind is the restraining of free-flowing thought. It is telling the carnal mind to "shush" when it would like to speak.

This isn't really all that difficult, but you will need to learn to keep a tight leash on your thoughts because there will always be that temptation for your mind to jump in and say, "But what if it doesn't work?" In those times, I just say to it, "Shut up! I'm not listening to you right now!" As I learned to shut out all thought for those few brief moments, it's almost as if I held my breath and just suspended time for a moment, without engaging any feelings, senses, or thoughts—just nothing.

In the process of doing nothing, I'm actually getting

myself out of the way so that God's Spirit can do what He does—the miracle of healing. When I prayed for Haley that first time, do you know what I felt when I prayed? Did I feel fire, tingling, or electricity flowing through my hands as I placed them on her in faith? No, I honestly felt nothing.

The only thing I needed to do was get my mind out of the way. This is the way you're going to get activated and begin to do the miraculous through the power of the Holy Spirit. This is the way it's all going to start. It's all going to start when you learn how to put the carnal mind in its place. You're going to learn how to firmly say to your carnal mind, "Just shut up and be silent right now. I'm going to let God do what He does." You don't have to focus. You don't have to think. All you need to do is speak in authority and then get out of the way.

THE CARNAL MIND AND THE ENEMY

When we can effectively quiet our carnal minds, we will stop believing the lies that have taken root there. We will also stop listening to its doubt and unbelief concerning the things of the Spirit. Understand that the carnal mind isn't trying to lie to you. It just is incapable of understanding the things of the Spirit. In fact, the carnal mind is so spiritually blind, that it is extremely susceptible to the thoughts and suggestions of the enemy.

The carnal mind doesn't think, "Oh, these thoughts are from the devil, so I should just ignore them," because the carnal mind cannot fully believe in the things that it cannot see (like the enemy) or understand them without physical evidence. It's easy for an enemy to fool you when you don't even believe he exists.

The realm of the natural mind is not equipped to fight in the realm of the spirit. Fighting the devil with our carnal mind is like going to a gun fight armed with a pea shooter! Your enemy loves to fight you in the realm of the natural because you have no supernatural strength or power when fighting from the resources of the old, natural, and carnal mind.

One instance where I really had to push the carnal mind aside while praying for someone's healing happened in May of 2015. I had the privilege to pray for a man named Jerry. Jerry was not only a non-Christian, but he was an atheist. He held no belief in God's existence at all.

I came across Jerry and a few of his friends hanging out at the Seattle Center, and I asked if any of them had any pain. Jerry reported that he'd recently injured his knee running, and that the pain level was about a five resting, and a seven when he applied pressure on it.

I prayed for Jerry, following the same pattern of the keys described in this book. After my first prayer, I asked Jerry to place weight on his knee. His response?

"It's a little better. Maybe."

I could see that he was still visibly favoring his opposite knee. I asked him to tell me honestly if there was still pain and he said yes.

While I'm not ever opposed to praying for the same

healing twice, this particular situation required all of my mental strength to force out the carnal mind. "Come on," it said. "This guy's unbelief is getting in the way!"

"Shut up," I told my mind. "Go away. Now." Just like a spirit fleeing, silence flooded my mind.

Then I prayed again, commanding the pain to get out now. Within seconds, a smile broke across Jerry's face.

"It's kind of ridiculous," he said. "I don't even believe in God or anything."

"You don't believe in God, but He loves you," I told him.

Jerry couldn't find any pain in his knee. See, the enemy can plant thoughts in our minds if we let him. He will watch our interactions with others and design a scheme against God's will using our own thoughts. Those lies must be harnessed and stopped so God's Spirit can lead the way.

EMBRACING CHRIST IN YOU

The first thing we must understand in unlocking the power of the kingdom is that we need to accept, affirm, and fully embrace without wavering that we are who and what God says we are. We need to know who and what we are according to God's Word. Let me say that again, because it cannot be over-emphasized. Not only are we who God says we are (regardless of anyone else's opinion), but we are also what God says we are.

Let's look now to God's written Word, the Bible,

and find out exactly who and what that is. In the end, your opinion and my opinion don't really matter. It is God's opinion alone that will stand.

> I have been crucified with Christ and I no longer live, but Christ lives in me. The life I now live in the body, I live by faith in the Son of God, who loved me and gave himself for me.
>
> — GALATIANS 2:20 NIV

The Bible makes it very clear: We are fully redeemed through the death and resurrection of Jesus. Our human weaknesses and imperfections have been washed away by the blood of our Savior. When we are thinking and living through His Spirit, it is as if we no longer live at all, but Christ is acting, thinking, talking, healing, and loving through us. Isn't that a beautiful promise?

Conversely, when we operate from our flesh, we make ourselves vulnerable to those same weaknesses and imperfections that Christ sacrificed to remove.

Imagine that you have a three-year-old son. He might have the best of intentions for you, but you probably wouldn't take tips from him on how to invest your money because he doesn't yet have a firm grasp or knowledge about how financial investments work. In the same way, you should never take spiritual direction from your carnal mind because it has no concept of spiritual things.

Knowing who you are and what you have is the solid rock of confidence that gives you the courage to step out in faith and do the miraculous. When you pray for big things, go all in. Your spirit mind can handle it. Your spirit mind can believe whatever God says. Don't compromise or settle for anything less than God's supernatural power. After I pray, I can give God time to work, shutting down the carnal mind and waiting on God. Then I must be brave enough to have it put to the test and honestly assessed for the results.

When you are a follower of Jesus Christ, then all of the keys to the kingdom have been given to you. They are accessible within you right now. Because we have connection and access to the mind of Christ right now, we are able to agree with the Word of God right now. That agreement is key to operating in the power of God's Spirit.

6

THE KEY OF WALKING IN THE SPIRIT MIND

If you were to attempt to wash your hands in a bucket of mud, it would be impossible for them to ever get free from the dirt you are attempting to remove. In the same way, if you are trying to pray from your spirit while allowing your natural, carnal mind to participate, you will be believing with one part of your inner-man while doubting with another part—completely ineffective. The only answer is to learn to tell the carnal mind to, "Shut up and be silent."

You have been given authority to speak over natural things as well as spiritual things.

In the Bible, Jesus cursed a fig tree and it withered from its roots upward. His disciples marveled that He had this kind of power by just speaking words to the tree. Jesus told them that this was not something that was unusual to those who operate from the spirit, but that they also could do these same things if they just had faith.

So Jesus answered and said to them, "Assuredly, I say to you, if you have faith and do not doubt, you will not only do what was done to the fig tree, but also if you say to this mountain, 'Be removed and cast into the sea,' it will be done."

— MATTHEW 21:21 NKJV

Don't miss the little truth that is contained in what Jesus said. When we read it, we usually just pick up part of the message that Jesus is saying. Jesus did not say, "If you have faith." Jesus said, "If you have faith *and do not doubt*." Faith wasn't His only focus. Having an absence of doubt was just as important.

Then Jesus said that you can speak to a mountain and it will obey you. That's pretty far out there, but if Jesus said it, I agree with it. If you think about it, your natural, carnal mind is a thing that is of this earth just like the mountain is. You have the authority to speak over that natural mind and command it to be silent and it will obey you.

MIND, SUBMIT TO SPIRIT

Once I was training a group in Montana and I was talking about quieting the carnal mind. After a break, a group of women returned to the meeting and asked if they could share something. One of the women said, "We are women, and we just can't stop our carnal mind from speaking. But we had a breakthrough during the break and we actually experienced silence in our minds for the first time!"

I asked them if they would share with us how they accomplished this. It was really quite simple—they used their authority to speak to their natural mind and command it to submit. This is what they said to themselves: "Mind, submit to my spirit. Spirit, take me to the Father." In that very moment they were instantly transported into the presence of God and their carnal minds were completely silent. You should try this for yourself. I have seen it help about 80 percent of the people who were having problems with silencing their carnal mind.

Your carnal mind will always be ready to reason with you about why God won't do a miracle. Your mind will tell you that the circumstances are not exactly right, or it isn't in His timing, or you aren't holy enough to wield such power, or that you have never heard of this kind of miracle happening before. It is the carnal mind that interferes with the performing of miracles, and until you address it, the miraculous will be stifled.

Take 18-year-old Taylor's story, for example. Taylor's mom phoned our church office and made an appointment to come in and have me pray for her son. Taylor is very tall and athletic, and as I recall, he had sustained his injuries while playing football. Taylor's mother had watched some of my YouTube videos, and after seeing them thought that rather than having extensive surgery, perhaps the Lord could heal Taylor miraculously.

One morning Taylor and his mother arrived at our church, and after introducing themselves, told me the specifics about Taylor's injury. Taylor had torn the labrum in both hips, was in constant pain, and was unable to participate in many physical activities. The only solution was to have surgery to rebuild each hip, and this would be followed by a long process of rehabilitation.

Taylor told me that he was famous on YouTube for doing amazing feats of memorization, and that if I filmed him, he would prefer that I did not use his stage name. I said, "Of course," and then I asked him to tell me what his pain level was. Then I had him demonstrate the limitations in his mobility.

His pain was about an eight out of 10. I prayed for Taylor using the method that the Lord had shown me, as described in this book. I prayed once and asked him to move the areas of the body that would normally cause him pain.

He did, but there was still some pain. He was not fully restored. In this moment, my carnal mind threatened to make its presence known. I could sense it at the edge of my spirit, and I pushed it away, silencing it.

Instead of letting doubt creep in, I leaned in to the Spirit of God and prayed again. After praying again, I asked Taylor to look for the pain. There wasn't any! Then I told Taylor to give it the full test, so he moved and jumped around. All of the pain was gone.

Taylor and his mother left and I didn't hear from

him again for about two months. Taylor had a surgery scheduled that was supposed to take place about a week after the time I prayed for him. The surgery was canceled because Taylor had been completely healed by the power of the Holy Spirit!

There are several YouTube videos of Taylor's healing on my page. Here are the titles in case you want to check them out: *Taylor gets Total Spiritual Overhaul – Jesus Heals! – Tom Loud* and *Taylor's Testimony of Healing 2 months later; The follow up!!! – Tom Loud.*

CLEANING OUT THE CLOSET

The devil cannot touch the spirit of a believer, but he certainly can drop thoughts into the carnal mind—doubts. Like he did in my earlier testimony involving Jerry.

It is these thoughts that are your Achilles heel when it comes to operating in faith and demonstration of power. When I discovered this truth, I began to pray with authority and then put a gag on my carnal mind so that all was quiet. I started to rest for a moment in God's presence.

Sometimes, before we will be able to discover what we really have, we will need to take on the task of figuratively "cleaning out the closet" of the wrong beliefs that are still stubbornly lingering in our natural, carnal mind. What I mean by that is, you often don't realize what you have within you until you discover it by intentionally evaluating and testing your thought patterns.

This is how you learn to walk in the mind of the spirit—the same way you learn and develop pretty much any other ability—you go out and put these things into practice.

It was a discipline I implemented when I met a man named Rodrick with pain in his right knee. He'd torn his ACL and also had a chipped kneecap. I told Rodrick that I was going to pray for him, and not only was the pain going to be healed, but the chip was going to go back into place.

Rodrick said, "No way."

But I knew better. With my carnal mind disengaged, my spirit mind was in control. My spirit mind knew that God would completely restore Rodrick's knee. My spirit mind simply accepts what God says as true. It does not question the reality of God's plain statements of truth. I hadn't started my healing ministry with that mindset. I set out on this journey knowing that God *could* provide complete restoration, but not *knowing with confidence* that He would.

I told Rodrick, "This is going to happen."

"Nope," he said.

My mind, now clear of doubt, never wavered because the carnal mind was disengaged. I didn't need to reason out how or why this was going to happen. I didn't need to think through all of the probable outcomes. This was going to happen simply because God said it would happen. He said He gave me authority to heal, and then He commanded me to go and heal. My born-again spirit is perfectly connected to and in tune with God's Spirit. My spirit does not question what God says.

Rodrick's pain level was about a seven when he moved his knee around. I told Rodrick I would pray for him and all he had to do was relax.

"Heavenly Father," I prayed, "Thank You for Rodrick. Thank You for who You are. I know that You love Rodrick and You made this appointment for him today because You don't want him in pain. I pray for this knee. I pray for the chip to go back into place right now. I command a new kneecap, muscles, tendons, and nerves. I command complete restoration right now—everything back into place like it was before the injury."

I paused a moment, with no engagement of the carnal mind, letting the Spirit work. Then I asked him how he felt.

"Nothing," he said.

"Test it out," I said. "Look for the pain. Tell me honestly how it feels."

He walked around a bit and looked confused. "No pain," he said. "None."

"Do you know how that's possible?"

"The good Lord."

Rodrick already knew Jesus as his Savior, but that day, he met Jesus as his healer.

THE NATURAL MIND VERSUS THE SPIRITUAL

The natural mind is something that not only has man been given, but that even animals possess. Their natural minds aren't as capable as ours, but they do have them and use them to operate in this world. The natural mind is guided by what it can see, sense, and rationalize based on the physical and natural world. People like the scientist Stephan Hawking develop their natural, rational, "carnal mind" to such a degree that they are able to look into some of the most complex scientific questions and theories of the modern age. But make no mistake about it, Mr. Hawking was absolutely oblivious to the things of the spiritual realm.

The word "carnal" as it is used in many translations of the Bible, simply means "flesh." If all you have to work from is the platform of your flesh and blood brain, then you will only be able to grasp the things of the natural and physical world. However, if you desire to understand the things of the invisible realm of the spirit, you are going to have to tap into the resources of the spiritual mind. This is not simply a mindset, as some believe. As a born-again believer, you actually possess a mind that can operate in the spiritual realm and can receive input and information from the very mind of God.

It's critically important that we understand the difference between "human" thinking and God's thoughts. When we can begin to recognize when the carnal mind is speaking and differentiate that from the mind of the Spirit, then we can begin to walk in the realm of kingdom power.

The problem with many of us is that we've let our natural mind take over the rule and control of our entire lives. We have allowed our natural mind to be seated on the throne of our heart, allowing the natural mind to make all of our decisions and rules. Therein lies the problem. This is why we are not walking in kingdom power as we should. Walking in kingdom power has absolutely nothing to do with the "carnal" mind.

The Bible says this in Romans 10:10 (KJV): "For with the heart man believeth unto righteousness; and with the mouth confession is made unto salvation."

We must note that this verse says, ". . . with the heart man believes." It does not say, ". . . with the mind man believes." This is because it is not with the mind that we have faith for salvation, but with the heart or "spirit." God has given us a body, a soul (which relates to the function of our natural mind), and a spirit. When the Bible talks about our "heart" in this context, it is not referring to our natural mind, but our spirit. We "believe" with our spirit (or "heart"), not with our natural mind.

I think you can begin to recognize in these verses that your natural, carnal mind has a different agenda in life than your spirit does. You also need to know that until you put your natural or "carnal mind" in its place (in subjection to the Spirit), then it is going to oppose you in everything you endeavor to do in your pursuit of walking in kingdom power.

GOD'S PROMISES ARE RIGHT NOW

Many of us have unwittingly held on to an Old Testament perspective on some things. Those beliefs and mindsets have covered up what Christ has already done for us and what He has already given us. Sometimes, we cling to beliefs that move all of the promises of God into the future. This places us into the unfortunate position of waiting for God to give us something that we have already been given.

Prior to the cross, many of the promises of God were in the future tense. But we must recognize that after the cross, many of those promises have already been fulfilled and we are no longer in the position of waiting for them. They are in our possession right now.

We can tell when we don't really believe we have these promises already, usually by the fact that we keep praying for God above to rain something down on us. We act like these are things that we are still waiting for. This points to the fact that we don't really believe that we have already received.

We pray for God to send down the anointing. We beg God to send down revival. The problem is that it doesn't work that way anymore under the New Covenant—the Covenant God made with us in the blood of His Son, Jesus.

God is no longer sitting up in yonder heaven, far out of our reach and view, but God is in our hearts and we are ever in His presence. The thought of God being way up yonder and far away is an Old Testament perspective. But that shouldn't be our perspective today.

One day I met a man named Carlos while he was out pouring concrete for work. Carlos told me that he had been in pain for twenty-five years in his back due to four bulging discs. He was in constant pain every day at a level of about seven or eight. I placed my hand on Carlos' back and spoke to the pain there. I spoke to the discs, the vertebrae, the spine. I told all of it be made whole and free of discomfort.

"I felt something," Carlos said as I finished my prayer.

I asked him to test out his back—the back that had kept him from living a normal life for almost three decades. I told him to be very honest and look for the pain.

He said, "I don't know . . ." He moved a bit more. "There's no pain."

I told him God loved him.

"I'm about to cry," Carlos said. And if you could see Carlos, you'd understand just how remarkable his reaction was. He was not a small man. Tough from days working manual labor.

People were walking by as tears streamed down his face. "I am not ashamed," he said.

Then, the greatest miracle of all, Carlos accepted the Lord as his Savior!

We don't need God to send us anything. Everything we need—and more—has already been provided. What we need is to accept *what is already ours*.

FROM THE FOOTSTOOL TO THE THRONE

In Isaiah 66:1, the Lord says that Heaven is His throne, and the earth is His footstool. To the people of Isaiah's time, it was appropriate to pray gazing up into Heaven saying, "The heavens, Oh Lord, are your throne and the earth is your footstool." This kind of imagery causes us to picture, in our mind's eye, the person who is offering the prayer as being way down here on earth (on the footstool), praying to a God way up in heaven, seated on an unapproachable throne. But that perspective has changed. Everything is different now since Jesus died on the cross.

Today, God lives within us and is seated on the throne of our hearts, and there is no distance or division between us. Not only is God living in our hearts, but as we've learned, we are seated with Him in heavenly places right now at this very moment.

> And God raised us up with Christ and seated us with Him in heavenly places in Christ Jesus, in order that in the coming ages He might show the incomparable riches of His grace, expressed in His Kindness to us in Christ Jesus. be done."
>
> — EPHESIANS 2:6-7 NIV

Today, in this post-cross era that we live in, our perspective isn't from the footstool (looking up to the throne). Rather, our view is from the throne looking down upon the earth (the footstool). As we see ourselves looking from the throne down to the earth, all the things we had previously considered as giants start to seem more like ants. That's the way God wants us to see things today—from that "throne" perspective.

So, we're going to have to change the way we think and we are going to have to align our view to reflect the New Testament, post-cross perspective. In fact, I'm going to tell you the truth—everything you think you are lacking in the realm of the Spirit—it's already yours.

CLAIMING YOUR NEW MIND

As I have stated previously, you have all of the keys to the kingdom already, but the problem is that you may not know how to use them. If you don't know how to use the keys, they are of no benefit and are useless to you. You will continue to live your life as those who don't have the keys at all.

Our minds are not bad, they're just not of the Spirit of God. The carnal mind has a legitimate function in our lives. It was given to man so that our bodies could properly function in the natural world. The natural and carnal mind maintains the functions of the blood flow to your heart and it operates all the vital systems in your body. It is also useful for figuring out problems that arise within the physical realm.

Your natural mind is what you utilize to work out mathematical problems and mechanical problems. It is good for figuring out how to fix your car, refrigerator, and washing machine, but it is not designed to perform spiritual tasks. But now that you understand that the greatest blockage or hindrance you have when it comes to walking or flowing in spiritual power is the blockage between your ears, you can make that critical change.

In Corinthians 2:14 (NASB) the Bible says, "But a natural man does not accept the things of the Spirit of God, for they are foolishness to him; and he cannot understand them, because they are spiritually discerned."

That doesn't need to be a problem for us, however, because we remember this important truth: "But we have the mind of Christ"(1 Corinthians 2:16b), and that mind is a spiritual mind that discerns and accepts the things of the spirit realm.

The fact of the matter is that once you become born-again of the Spirit, you get a new mind. When I say you get a new mind, I'm not saying the old mind is no longer present, because obviously it is. And the challenge is that the old mind is still objecting and interfering with the things of the Spirit. I am not saying that once you receive Christ, your natural mind is done away with. Instead, I am saying that when you receive Christ into your heart, you get a new mind. You can choose to *use that new mind in your spiritual walk* or you can allow your natural mind to continue to run your life, just as it did prior to your salvation.

If you allow your natural and carnal mind to remain in control of your life, it will keep you walking out your born-again life without faith and power. The result is that you will be living a life that looks no different from anyone else born into this natural world.

WHEN TO STOP PRAYING

It's time to ask yourself this question: "Did Jesus or His followers live a normal life that looked no different from the rest of the world, or did they lead lives marked by the miraculous, the unexplainable, and the remarkable?"

The problem with many believers is that they don't have any of their own real-life, personal experiences of seeing God move in a powerful, supernatural way. They don't have the experiences that those who followed Christ had in the New Testament. It is apparent that those early Christians experienced the miraculous quite frequently in their day-to-day lives.

The reason many Christians don't have these types of supernatural experiences is largely because they are operating only out of their carnal mind and not out of the nature of the "new man" (Ephesians 4:22).

In order to identify your old nature (your old way of thinking) and begin to think in a new way, let's look at a few scriptures together.

Ephesians 1:3 says, "Blessed be the God and Father of our Lord Jesus Christ, who has blessed us in Christ with every spiritual blessing in the heavenly places."

Think of it this way: We find ourselves sometimes praying, "Lord, please give us this gift, give us that blessing, give us this revelation, and give us this ability," and God is saying, "Wake up, it's already in you!"

It's kind of like we are saying, "God, send us the download," and He's saying, "You already got the download, just open the file!" Once you "open the file" (acknowledge what you have already been given), then you will find everything in it that you need. When you begin to recognize what you already have, then you'll stop praying for it.

THE MIND OF A ZEBRA

I often ask people if they have ever seen someone riding a zebra. The answer is usually no. The reason behind this is very important. While a zebra looks like a horse, the two are very different.

A wild horse can be captured and an experienced rider can "break" that horse. Breaking a horse is a matter of breaking its will so that it will submit to being ridden. When the rider gets on the back of the wild horse, its instinct is to try to buck off the rider immediately. After a while, the horse surrenders and submits itself to the rider. A broken horse is now a servant to man and not just an uncontrollable, wild beast.

Zebras may look like horses but they are not the same. A zebra cannot be broken. A zebra will never submit to a rider, but will buck and buck until it drops dead. You can't break a zebra and you cannot make the carnal mind yield or submit to God's Word.

What you can do is switch over to the spirit mind instead.

You could try to ride the zebra of your carnal mind for the rest of your life, but it will never submit to functioning in obedience to God's Word or to the leading of the Holy Spirit. Maybe this word picture will help the next time you're in a situation where you need to disengage your carnal mind and walk in your spirit mind instead: Get off of the zebra. Get on the horse.

WHAT IS SPIRITUAL WARFARE, REALLY?

All of the issues and difficulties we have in trying to walk in the Spirit-filled life are related to the lack of control we have over our carnal mind. Take fear for example. God did not give you the spirit of fear, but of power, love, and a sound mind (2 Timothy 1:7). All of these wonderful things exist in the mind of Christ, the mind of the new man and not in the carnal mind.

Could it be that we are not winning these spiritual battles because we're doing it all wrong? Because really, if we were doing it the right way, shouldn't we have succeeded by now?

Have you ever wondered how much good our spiritual warfare is actually doing? Some of us have been wrestling against the same problems for several years and are yet to overcome them. I want you to look with me at the Scriptures concerning the fight, war, and the conflict that we have in this world—the fight that we face against our enemy, the devil.

For we do not wrestle against flesh and blood, but against the rules, against the authorities, against the cosmic powers over this present darkness, against the spiritual forces of evil in heavenly places.

— EPHESIANS 6:12 ESV

We wrestle not against flesh and blood. However, we do wrestle. So what is it that we do wrestle against? ". . . but against the rulers, against the authorities, against the cosmic powers over this present darkness, against the spiritual forces of evil in the heavenly places."

It is plainly expressed here that our wrestling match is not one of flesh against flesh, but our wrestling opponent is a spirit. And if we are to effectively fight against this spirit, we need to learn how to fight *from the spirit* and *in the spirit*.

For far too long people have misunderstood what spiritual warfare actually looks like. Let's find out what it's really all about by looking at 2 Corinthians 10:3-6 (NKJV): "For though we walk in the flesh, we do not war according to the flesh. For the weapons of our warfare are not carnal but mighty in God for pulling down strongholds, casting down arguments and every high thing that exalts itself against the knowledge of God, bringing every thought into captivity to the obedience of Christ."

This passage tells the believer that we do have weapons and we do have warfare, but it says the weapons of our warfare are not natural or carnal, but they're mighty through God. So, we know we have an enemy. We know we have weapons and we know we are engaged in warfare. That is all very plain, isn't it?

We are all going to have to fight the devil, and fortunately for us, our weapons are mighty. That sounds pretty good, doesn't it? We are also told our weapons are so mighty that they can pull down strongholds. That sounds great, doesn't it? So, with all of that in mind, now you can begin to see yourself armed with these awesome weapons, and with them you can slice and dice devils right and left. That's how we typically interpret these words, right?

But listen again to what it really says: "For the weapons of our warfare are not carnal, but they're mighty through God to the pulling down of strongholds." And what are these strongholds that we're pulling down?

Imaginations.

What?

The weapons we have are designed not to destroy demons, but to destroy *imaginations*? Do you mean the imaginations that are in our natural mind? Let's continue on and see what else these weapons can powerfully accomplish through our warfare.

". . . and every high thing that exalts itself above the knowledge of God." These mighty weapons destroy the strongholds of a type of knowledge which places itself above the knowledge of God. That's the kind of knowledge that's in your head. This knowledge is the kind that has been placed there by man's teaching that goes contrary to God's, and by the lying suggestions of your enemy—the devil.

Teachings such as "man evolved from the ape"—that false knowledge is taught in schools as a fact and as a scientific truth. But that kind of knowledge stands in opposition to God's knowledge, as expressed in His Word.

The knowledge that is found in God's Word tells us that God created man in His image and likeness. God is certainly not an ape! Man often places his own knowledge over God's, but only one can be true. Well, these mighty weapons of warfare that have been given to us are for the purpose of casting down all of that false knowledge which has been implanted through false teaching and now resides in your natural (carnal) mind.

Let's go a little further in this verse and see what else these "mighty weapons" are capable of doing.

"Bringing into captivity every thought into the obedience of Christ."

Once again, these weapons are battling against and taking captive thoughts. And where do these thoughts reside? They reside in the carnal mind, the mind of the old man, and the mind of the flesh.

The big wrestling match that you are facing is in your head, and we need to learn how to step out of the arena of the carnal mind because that's where the devil fights his battles with you. Instead of fighting against a malevolent spirit with the weaknesses of the natural mind, we need to learn to step into the mind of Christ, where the enemy has no power due to the fact that in Christ, you have been given the ultimate authority over your enemy.

When you put on the mind of Christ, there's no longer any fight. The fight is over because in Christ, you are already the victor. In the mind of the spirit, (the mind of the new man), you are already an overcomer and your enemy has no power. In fact, he's been put under your feet.

GODLIKE FAITH

Have you ever wondered what kind of faith God has? Is it like our faith? It's not like our faith at all. But we can have Godlike faith. In Mark 11:22 (NKJV) Jesus said, "Have faith in God." Upon closer examination of this verse, some scholars note that it could more accurately be rendered, "Have the faith of God." In fact, some modern versions such as the Young's Literal Translation and the Douay-Rheims Bible render it that way: "faith of God." God has His own brand of faith and I don't want a knock-off. I want the kind He has. Don't you?

I want you to consider something right now. God has never had a new thought. Think about that for a minute. You and I have a creative process with our thoughts. That process has a beginning and an end. It takes time. God has no such process. He has all knowledge immediately. It is not hinged on time, and no process is necessary.

Sometimes we think about our Creator and we

picture God as if He was just like us. In reality, He's quite a bit different than we are in the way He thinks and operates. We picture Him as someone who, perhaps in eternity-past, was just sitting all alone in this place of emptiness and one day said to Himself, "Hmm, what should I create? Perhaps I'll create . . . Umm, let's see. Some planets! Yeah, that's it! And I'll put some people on them, and animals and trees. That's a great idea. That's what I'll do!"

Nothing like that ever happened because everything that has ever come to God's mind has always been in God's mind. Nothing has ever been a new thought to Him. He has known everything from the beginning. There is no process that His mind needs to work through. It's all simply knowledge to Him. He knows what's going to happen a million years from now and He knows what happened a million years ago. It's all the same to Him. He stands outside of time and everything in His mind is simply truth. Knowledge. Fact.

When you learn to operate from the mind of the Spirit, you don't need to learn everything. You just need to know what the facts are according to God's Word. If we could accept God's Word as fact, then it would not be necessary for us to try to believe or have faith for it. I have been taught that there are radio waves in the air right in front of me, even though I cannot see them or sense them. I don't try to believe in them. I simply accept them as facts based on my trust in the word of scientists who have fully researched the subject and proven it. I didn't do the research myself. I just accepted their word for it. When I first learned about radio waves, I didn't have to try to believe for it, I just counted it as a fact.

So why do we have to try to believe God's Word? Why can't we just count it as fact based on the reliability of the one who said it? Real faith (God's faith) is not a matter of a process. It is a full acceptance of what God has said as being an absolute fact.

CHILDLIKE FAITH

The Bible talks about something that is called "childlike faith" and it can be found in Luke chapter 18. This is a kind of faith that is powerful and effective. It is pure and doesn't have any doubt mixed in. This is the kind of faith that can receive the things of the kingdom.

So, what does the faith of a child look like? It looks like this: A parent tells his child that there is a fat man in a red suit who flies around in a sleigh pulled by eight tiny reindeer. He also goes on to say that once a year, this man carries a bag big enough to deliver gifts to every child in the whole world and he is able to accomplish this task in one night. The child believes it without question. Why? Because the child looks up to their parent and trusts that they know what they're talking about. They believe that their parents' words are trustworthy.

They believe this outrageous story without needing to have explained to them any of the obvious problems and impossibilities, such as the lack of aerodynamics of the sleigh, the lack of thrust of the reindeer, or the impractical immensity and weight of a bag large enough to carry toys for every child on earth.

The child requires no explanation. The fact that it was told to them by their parent is all the proof they need in order to believe.

In this analogy, there is an obvious problem. Parents can be wrong and parents can lie. Later in life, the child learns of the fallibility of their parent and then begins to ask questions rather than blindly believing everything their parent says.

However, this shouldn't be the problem that we have with believing what our Heavenly Father says to us in His Word. It shouldn't pose a problem because, unlike a human parent, God the Father has never lied and has never been wrong. The Father wants us to believe His Word like a little child would. We believe what He says without need of explanation because we have complete confidence in the One who said it. This is childlike faith. It is pure, unwavering, and incredibly powerful.

I met a Seventh Day Adventist once named Josephine. Josephine preferred I not lay hands on her. Because I had faith that God could heal her regardless of whether or not I touched her, I shrugged and said, "He will still heal you."

Josephine had pain in her shoulder due to a slipped disc in her neck. Her pain at the time I met her was about a five. I told her I would use a shadow to pray for her and that God was going to remove the pain. I stated it as fact because it was a fact.

I spoke to the muscles, tendons, ligaments, and vertebrae to move back into the correct place. I commanded that the pain leave at that moment. When I was finished, I asked Josephine to test out her neck and shoulder.

"What did you do to me?" she asked. "The pain is gone."

"What do you think about that?" I asked her.

"Is it psychological?" she asked me, trying to logically deduce how the pain had left her body.

"No," I replied. "Josephine, Jesus told the apostles they'd do greater works than He did. You don't know it yet, but since you have Jesus in you, you could do this too. All that is required is faith."

The natural mind has issues with believing God's Word. This is because it has a hard time accepting as fact things that it cannot see or sense. It has a problem with the things that have been declared to be true in God's Word when they cannot be seen or sensed by the natural senses. Just like the radio waves, whether you believe it or not, God is real, alive, and present. And His Word is true.

Here's the difference between trying to believe the things of God with the carnal mind and actually believing them with the mind of the spirit. When you work out of the spirit mind, you don't have to wrestle with things such as, "Oh, how does that work? Let me get a full understanding of how that works. Let me decide how that can be possible. I mean really, how can that possibly happen?"

When we think in this way with the carnal mind rather than the mind of the Spirit, we find ourselves getting stuck in the quagmire of *trying to figure stuff out* before we can accept, receive, or believe it. That just isn't the way it works for God—He just knows.

Can you imagine this kind of faith, where you begin operating in the mind of Christ and that mind completely agrees with the Word of God? The mind of Christ has no argument or disagreement with the Word of God whatsoever. Rather, it is complete and unquestioning agreement with God's Word because the mind of Christ understands that the Word of God is simply fact and not theory. It is not opinion or wishful thinking. It is just unquestionable fact.

Can you imagine if you operated out of that mindset? Imagine that you could just look at the Word of God and say, "Oh, the Word says this. It's just fact and there's no process necessary. I don't have to understand it. I don't have to think about it."

It's as if you had a math test and all of the answers after the equal sign were already filled in and you didn't have to work through them. You just read the equation out loud, "Two plus two equals four. There it is. That's settled."

That's what it looks like when you are operating in pure faith. Godlike faith. Pure faith is simply operating from the mind of Christ that is already in complete agreement with the Word of God.

7

THE KEY OF CALLING

In 2 Corinthians 9:8 (NLT) the Bible says, "And God is able to bless you abundantly, so that in all things at all times, having all that you need, you will abound in every good work."

I would call healing people a good work. I would call delivering people a good work. God's Word says that we have already received everything we need to abound in every good work. But first, we must believe that not only is this calling ours, but that this calling is possible.

YOU HAVE BEEN CALLED

Jesus preached the truth, but He wasn't the only one who came claiming to be the Messiah. Why would people believe Him over others who preached different "truths"? Because Jesus was able to back up His words with actions—miracles, signs, and wonders.

Here's what Jesus said about miraculous works: "But if I do them, even though you do not believe me, believe the works, that you may know and understand that the Father is in me and I am in the Father" (John 10:38 NIV).

The gospel that we are supposed to declare will not be believed by many if our gospel is simply words. As Jesus demonstrated, the words should be accompanied by the demonstration of God's power.

Some are called to be apostles, some are called to be pastors, some teachers, and others are called to be evangelists. But all are called to be ambassadors who have been authorized to carry God's power wherever they go. His kingdom is not just demonstrated in words, but in signs and wonders as well.

Here's what Paul had to say on this subject: "My message and my preaching were not with wise and persuasive words, but with a demonstration of the Spirit's power" (1 Corinthians 2:4 NIV).

We may not share in a specific calling such as teaching or evangelism as being the primary gifting and anointing God has for us, but we all share the calling to be disciples. And this is how a disciple demonstrates the validity of God's Word: "Then the disciples went out and preached everywhere, and the Lord worked with them and confirmed his word by the signs that accompanied it" (Mark 16:20 NIV).

So, who is called to perform these types of signs and wonders? You are! We are all called to do good works in the name of Jesus.

A NEW CREATION IN CHRIST

You may say, "I've done some really bad things in my life. I've ruined my ministry. I can't be used now." But this is not biblical.

> Therefore, if anyone is in Christ, the new creation has come: The old has gone, the new is here!
>
> — 2 CORINTHIANS 5:17 NIV

When we were born-again from above, we became a new creation. In fact, if you look up the word for "new creation" found in 2 Corinthians 5:17, you will find that it is the Greek word, *ktisis*, which is translated as "creation." It literally means, "A new creature, always of divine work." Did you hear that? We became a new creature—a different type of creature than we had ever been before!

You may again argue that the unfortunate sins holding you back from doing good works are sins that you committed *after* salvation. But you're talking about your flesh—a flesh that can be forgiven by leaning into the grace of the Holy Spirit.

In the beginning, man was originally made in the image and likeness of God, but then man fell. When man failed to keep God's commandment, that perfect and glorious image which he had been given became tarnished. Its glory was damaged. But that all changes when we are joined to Christ.

When we repent from our old life of sin and disobedience, turn to Christ, and invite Him to make His home in our heart, that image of fallen man is restored. We experience a wonderful transformation. We don't simply become a better person, but a different person. We become brand new! When He restores that image we were originally designed to carry, the old man passes away and a new man rises up to take his place.

You are not "too far gone" to be of use in the kingdom because the power of the living God is within you. His mind is within you. His heart is within you. *This* is who you truly are—God's redeemed child. Through the power of God, the sins of the flesh vanish when we repent.

This miraculous transformational power of God's Holy Spirit instantaneously makes us a new creation, a new man. The new creation is the kind of creation that carries the same spiritual DNA as our Heavenly Father. This new creation is no longer like that of the old, fallen man, but in fact, is divine in origin. We who were once sinners separated from God have now become sons and daughters of God.

GOD'S OWN HEART

Grace and peace be multiplied to you in the knowledge of God and of Jesus our Lord, as His divine power has given to us all things that *pertain* to life and godliness, through the knowledge of Him who called us by glory and virtue, by which have been given to us exceedingly great and precious promises, that through these you may be partakers of the divine nature, having escaped the corruption that is in the world through lust.

— 1 PETER 1:2-4 NKJV

This verse tells us that we are "partakers of His divine nature." That means that instead of having the nature of fallen man, we have the nature of our divine Father. This new man has new desires. This new man has a new heart.

Without having God's divine nature, I would have never been able to minister to a pair of friends I met at a skate park—both named David!

The first David I spoke to told me he had severe pain in his left ankle that was at about a level eight. Instead of touching his ankle, I placed my hand above it, casting a shadow over the area that hurt. When I finished, I asked him to look for the pain.

"It's totally gone," he said.

"What do you think about that?" I asked.

"My mind is blown," he said. Judging from the astounded look on his face, I believed him!

After praying for his ankle, I prayed for his kneecap too. Of course God healed that as well. David hopped back on his skateboard and raced away.

His friend, the other David, had been watching the whole time. "Hey, I've got pain too."

After praying for his ankle, he actually took his foot in his own hand and bent it every direction. He laughed. "Man, it's gone!"

Believe it or not, a third skater came up to us and lifted his pant leg. "Can you heal this?" he asked.

"Yes," I told him. "God will heal you." This third guy's name was Elijah—what a great name! Elijah had a busted kneecap. I prayed for him and then asked him how he felt.

"I don't know," he said, eyes closed as he tested his knee for pain. "It sort of feels peaceful."

"Be really honest," I told him.

Elijah gave it the ultimate test—popping a few tricks on his skateboard.

"It's fine now," he said.

"No pain?"

"No pain, lots of gain," he said and skated off.

I went on to pray for several more of their friends that day. This is all made possible by me having God's divine nature living right on the inside of me. The Bible says you have it too!

The Bible says that in these last days, God will take out our heart of stone and give us a new heart. In Ezekiel 11:19 (NIV) the Bible says, "I will give them an undivided heart and put a new spirit in them; I will remove from them their heart of stone and give them a heart of flesh."

We have a new heart—a heart after, or like, God's heart. It's a heart that loves the things that God loves and hates the things that God hates. We must begin to embrace the reality that we are made in the image and likeness of our Heavenly Father. To say otherwise is to call God a liar.

WHAT YOU ARE MADE TO DO

Two questions that have plagued philosophers for thousands of years are these: What is the meaning of life? and What is the key to true happiness? The key to happiness cannot be found in this world because it is not from this world. The key to happiness is found when we become who God created us to be, which includes doing the things that God has called us to do. You will never find happiness or fulfillment in life until you are doing the things you were made to do.

Let me give you this analogy. Suppose you take a racehorse and you harness him up to a plow and force him to pull the plow. It's a lot of work for him because he was not bred for that kind of work. He may be able to do it, but it's very hard labor and a real struggle for him. Another thing that will soon become apparent is that the racehorse doesn't particularly enjoy the work—he wasn't bred to pull a plow, he was bred to run fast.

Now suppose you take a plow horse and put him on a race track and try to make him run as fast as he can. This will be a challenge for him because he wasn't bred to run fast, he was bred to pull a plow. On the other hand, let's talk about that racehorse again. If you take the racehorse and you put him on a track and you make him run all out, do you know what you will discover?

Though he is covered with sweat and has expended a lot of energy, he loves to run fast. He loves to run because that is what he was made for. It suits him, and he can't wait to get out on the track and run like the wind.

This principle also applies to the new man. It applies to the sons and daughters of God. The new man is made to be like God. You were made to carry out God's plan in this world. You were made to carry out God's will. Only when you are doing what you were made to do will you find true fulfillment, purpose, and happiness.

When you continue to live the carnal life of the old man, it is impossible to find peace and satisfaction. You don't put new wine into old wineskins or they will burst. When you try to live the old man's life through the new creation reality, you will be struggling against your new nature. Pain and disappointment will be your reward.

Many of us only remember our past. We remember the person we were before we got saved and we think, "The old me only likes this or only likes that." But when you pursue those things, you find out they no longer satisfy you. This is because your heart has been changed —you have been rewired. The things you used to desire in the past are no longer able to satisfy you.

Now that you have been made a new creation, things that you wouldn't have even considered doing before are actually the things that get you excited. What kind of things? Things like going out and praying for people, witnessing to people, doing the good works that Christ demonstrated and told us that we would do also.

THE NEW WAYS OF THE NEW MAN

Those scary, foreign, and strange activities that you are sure God has called someone else to do will actually bring you an amazing degree of joy, excitement, and passion for the things of God. The new you is made for these things, and if you will resist the mind of the flesh which is controlled by the old man, you will discover that you can thrive in doing the good works you were called to do.

When you are doing what you were made to do, fulfillment is your constant companion. You might be saying to yourself right now, "I don't think doing those scary, radical, and extreme things will really make me happy." That's your problem. You're "thinking" again. The new man is led by the Spirit, not by the natural, carnal mind. Go ahead, give it a try! You will never know if what I am saying is true until you have actually tried it for yourself.

I take people out all the time who say, "I don't know if I can approach people. I don't know if I can pray for people." Let me share a story with you that speaks to those doubts.

I take people out to train in marketplace ministry every week, but on this particular day, I took a skeptic with me. Often, I take trainees to a bus depot nearby because there are so many people there who have nothing to do but wait. It is easy to begin a conversation with the idle!

I suspect my skeptic friend felt that spending his day

at a bus depot praying for people did not sound wildly entertaining. Boy, was he wrong! We approached a young man named Brandon, and I asked him if he had any pain in his body. He said, "Yes, I always have pain."

Then he told us his story. Brandon had been born with an unusual birth defect called lumbar vertebra defect. He explained to us that this meant he was born with an extra vertebra in his spine, causing great pain. In fact, he told us that he had never experienced a single day in his life without pain.

I informed Brandon that we would pray for him and that God would heal him—removing all pain. This of course sounded impossible, but he knew he had nothing to lose. I instructed my skeptical friend to put his hand on Brandon's back and to repeat the words I spoke to him.

He complied and did exactly as I instructed him, then removed his hand. I then asked Brandon to move about and search for the pain. Brandon began to bend and twist and had a puzzled expression on his face. I asked, "Is there any pain"?

He said, "No!"

Then I asked, "Is this the first time in your whole life that you have ever experienced having no pain?"

He said, "Yes!"

I then asked him if he knew why that happened, and he said he did not. So I told him it was because God loved him and wanted to be part of his life, and then we continued to talk to him about salvation in Jesus Christ.

As for my skeptical friend? He was no longer a

skeptic! In fact, he continued to accompany me on many trips to the bus depot after his interaction with Brandon. He had no idea how much he would enjoy performing the miraculous works of Christ until he tried it for himself.

My *formerly* skeptical friend is not the only one. I've taken many doubters or hesitant people out to pray for others. I don't listen to their initial protests anymore, because I have been through it so many times before. I realize that before they go out, they just don't know what they don't know.

After they go out and experience these things, they often turn to me and say something like, "Wow! I never realized what I have this whole time! This is fun. This is exciting. This is fulfilling." And that is when they begin to realize what they were made to do.

The new man is made to do the good works of God that Jesus modeled to His apostles. The new man is made to minister to others. He is made to reach out to the lost and the hurting, and to demonstrate the love of the Father to them. That's what the new man is made for. That's the way that Jesus reaches people today— through average believers like you and me. When you start doing what you're made to do, you find fulfillment and happiness. Watch out, because you just may get hooked!

WHO AM I CALLED TO HEAL?

It's much harder to see anyone healed without compassion. Do I mean that you have to have a warm feeling in your heart for the person that you're praying for? No.

Do I mean that you have to experience a certain emotion for the person you're praying for? No.

I mean that if you don't have compassion for other human beings, you will stay at home and do nothing. Compassion gets you moving!

It is a wonderful honor to lead someone into relationship with Jesus. Regardless of everything else you've accomplished in ministry, introducing someone to the Savior is the ultimate highlight. As you watch my videos on YouTube, you'll notice that often the people that I'm praying for are surprised at the results. In fact, they are often in shock!

I love to see the surprised look on their face because that's what tells me that they weren't expecting it. If they weren't expecting it, then it cannot be a matter of their mind simply believing something. That is to say, it cannot be the power of suggestion at work. I've actually prayed for people that said they don't believe in Jesus or healing, and much to their amazement, they were healed anyway.

People ask me the question: "Can you pray for somebody who says they don't believe?" Absolutely! God shows Himself powerfully so that the unbelieving will realize who He is. There is an erroneous teaching out there which has been taught for years. It says, "If the person you are praying for has any doubt, the healing won't occur."

That is patently false! That teaching is taught by those who have provided themselves a way to escape when things don't work out.

For example, they will pray in faith for someone to be healed, and when nothing happens, they say, "That's because you didn't have enough faith!" Jesus never did that, so I never do that.

I have prayed for atheists who have challenged me, telling me that nothing would happen, and still, they have been healed. I don't need their faith to help me because mine alone is enough. It doesn't matter who has faith in any healing as long as there is at least one who has faith.

8

FISHING FOR PEOPLE

The primary focus of this book is the demonstration of God's power through the three things that Jesus taught His disciples to do: preach the kingdom, heal the sick, and cast out demons. But for the sake of getting people started, I have primarily focused on ministering in healing, signs, and wonders. Through the same discipline of shutting off the chatter of the carnal mind, it is possible to begin walking in prophetic words and in words of knowledge as well.

You can talk to anyone operating in these gifts and you will find that an important aspect of speaking out God's personal messages to people involves just opening the mouth and speaking out, without ever engaging the thought processes. The messages that God gives are not received by the focus and concentration of the natural mind but by suspending the natural mind's function and engaging the Spirit alone. This is also the case when it comes to praying in tongues—the natural mind is not engaged.

This is what the Apostle Paul said about praying in tongues. In 1 Corinthians 14:14 (NIV) he said, "For if I pray in a tongue, my spirit prays, but my mind is unfruitful." When a person is praying in an unknown tongue, their speech is flowing from the mouth, but the natural mind is not the source of the words. They come from the spirit.

Speaking out a prophetic word, or word of knowledge from the Lord, often happens this same way. You just start moving your mouth and words come out. You do not even know what's going to come out until it does. When the utterance emerges from your lips, you are hearing it for the first time along with everyone present.

When I speak a word from the Spirit to someone, they may say, "Wow, how did you know that about me?" It pours out without any forethought because it flows directly from God's Spirit to my spirit and then out of my mouth.

You are a son or a daughter of God and you have been given His authority. He wants you to use it for the good of the kingdom. For this reason, your spoken words carry power. All of creation—natural and spiritual—is subject to your words spoken in faith.

Sometimes, when ministering healing, something strange will manifest— something that we need to address. There are times when you will command an infirmity to be healed, and instead of going away, it moves. Numerous times I have seen people being prayed for that had a problem with one knee and the pain left that knee and then manifested in the other. In cases like these, there are often demonic spirits involved. This is not something to be alarmed about—demons are subject to your commands just as much as sickness and infirmity are subject to your commands.

If you sense that a demonic spirit is involved, command it to leave in Jesus' name. Sometimes, they try to resist. In those cases I will speak a bit more firmly as if I were giving a command to a disobedient dog. In these situations, you are the master and the spirit must obey you. Never fear demons. If you do, they will recognize that you really don't know who you are and don't realize the authority you carry. On the other hand, if you know who you are and you enter a room full of witches and occultists, the scariest person in the room is you.

A RESPONSIBILITY AND AN HONOR

Every time I go out, I see people healed. If I don't go out, not only will I not see a miracle, but someone who could have received a life-changing miracle will have to continue suffering. There is one day a week that I have set aside to go out alone or with a group and do marketplace ministry, whether I feel like it or not.

If you wait until you feel like it, then the enemy will

do everything in his power to make it difficult for you to ever feel like it. This is like exercising a spiritual muscle. If you will do it faithfully with regular use, you will grow stronger and stronger.

Every day that I just decide to do nothing, that I don't feel like going out, that's a day that somebody stays in misery or stays lost. I am not saying this to make you feel guilty, but quite the opposite. The fact that you have the power to change lives for now and eternity should get you excited.

You carry inside you the answer to every lost person's need. You can bring deliverance to those who are bound. You can bring hope to the hopeless. You have the answer that someone out there is searching for.

In a real sense, you are the "superhero" that brings the world of the impossible into reality. Jesus' life, death, and resurrection changed our world forever. Now He sends you and me. We bring the life-changing words and we bring the life-changing power to those in need.

There is no greater honor than being an instrument in God's hands to turn people towards the Savior and lead them into eternal life.

Yes, that's a heavy responsibility. But oh, what an honor!

That is what it feels like if you will step out of your comfort zone and into the miracle of God's power.

What could be more exciting? What could be more important?

Doing good works in the name of God is one of the most important things that we have all been called to do.

Someone is out there right now. They are hurting and lost and you hold the keys to their new life in your hands. If Jesus calls us to do this, why would we not do it?

GO WHERE THE FISH ARE

When I take people out for training in marketplace ministry, I tell them that we are going "fishing".

Jesus saw some men mending their nets by the Sea of Galilee and called to them saying, "Come, follow me."

What do you suppose they thought He was going to do with them? Was He going to tell them that if they followed Him, He would make them successful businessmen?

That He would make them rich?

That He would make them powerful like a king or governor?

That He would make them into scholars?

No, Jesus told them exactly what He intended to do with them, and this is what He said:

"Come, follow me," Jesus said, "and I will send you out to fish for people."

— MATTHEW 4:19 NIV

This is the greatest calling of any man—the greatest good work.

As I said, I tell the people I am training, "I am going to take you fishing."

I know where the best fishing hole is and I know how to catch fish. So I can promise them this—we will *find* fish, but we have no idea what our net will pull up. I can't tell them how many we will catch, or what kind we will catch, or even if we will catch one fish. But one thing I can promise is that if they never go out where the fish are and drop their net, they *definitely will not* catch any fish.

I am telling you the same thing.

It doesn't matter to the Father how many fish you catch on any given day, but that you are faithful to go out and fish.

The idea of going several miles inland and setting up a fish trap on dry land, waiting for some fish to wander into your trap is not the best way to fish. But this is what most people do in Christianity. They build a nice church, they set up an attractive fish trap, and they wait for some unsuspecting fish to wander in and get caught.

If you want to catch fish, you need to go where the fish are. They're not usually in church, so you need to go and find them where they live.

Marketplace ministry is the name we give to the act of reaching out to the lost and praying for their needs physically, emotionally, and psychologically in public. This is the same model that the apostles and disciples of Jesus demonstrated from the very beginning of the church age. They did what Jesus did because it works.

It's time to pick up where they left off. It's now time

for the church—not just the TV personalities but the average Christian like you and me—to get out of the pew and work in the field. Because the harvest is ripe and ready to be reaped.

GOOD WORKS IN ACTION

I often get asked, "What do you do before you go out to minister to people?" My answer is always the same: I start my day off with prayer.

Prayer is how we get to the mind of the Father. It's also how to invite His partnership in everything we attempt to do for His kingdom. Prayer is the foundation of every effective spiritual endeavor that we will embark on. No prayer, no power, no direction.

In 2 Timothy 4:2 (NIV) the Bible says, "Preach the word; be prepared in season and out of season; correct, rebuke and encourage; with great patience and careful instruction."

The King James Version puts it like this: "Be instant, in season and out."

We need to be ready to minister at a moment's notice whenever the opportunity arises. I am prepared to minister to people any time of day. But if I'm going to intentionally go out and minister to people, I like to pray first.

I also like to read some Scripture as well. God's Word inspires me in what I am about to do. Combining His Word with prayer is a powerful combination.

Then, I purpose in my heart that I'm going to go out

and do whatever God and His Holy Spirit direct me to do. I know that whoever God puts before my path is fair game. In this mode, I am ready and willing to pray for anybody, at any time, and in any place.

The second question I get is: "How do you approach people?" First, I keep in mind that when I approach them, I am a stranger. This can make people uncomfortable and suspicious. So I normally introduce myself by name. This helps put people at ease.

Then I ask, "Can I pray for you? Do you have any pain in your body?" It's kind of weird to people who have never encountered such things.

As you approach a person you're looking to pray for, walk up with a gentle smile on your face. Now, be careful that your smile doesn't look scary or forced. That can be off-putting as well.

With a reasonably sane-looking smile on your face, simply ask them a question with the same kind of casual ease that you would have if you were asking them for the time. Only this time, you say, "Excuse me, Hi. My name is _____. We are out here today praying for people and God is healing them. Do you have any pain in your body?"

There are only three responses you usually have to deal with: "Yes," "No," or, "I'm not interested."

When the answer is "Yes," we walk through that open door and gather further information so that we can address their specific needs. When the answer is "No," do not assume that means that they don't want prayer. That could mean that they don't have any pain.

UNLOCKING KINGDOM POWER

When the answer is anything like "I'm not interested," just say, "God bless you," and move on. Don't force open a closed door. They are not ready.

FINDING FISH

When you're shopping in a store, you can get yourself accustomed to maintaining a state of heightened awareness of things around you. As you become aware of the people around you, you are always poised for the Holy Spirit to draw your attention to someone that He wants you to reach out and minister to. Sometimes, the greatest ability that will make you a prime candidate to be used by God is *availability*.

Until this becomes your norm, it may seem difficult to break the ice and approach that first person of the day. It's a bit like getting into a cold pool of water. At first you put your toe in and say, "Oh, no, this is really cold. I don't know if I really want to do this!" Instead, if you throw yourself in all at once, you'll find that you acclimate right away.

I will walk up to any person—it doesn't matter what they look like. They can look like the type of person that would reject you right away, but don't be guided by outward appearances. They could be the type of person that looks hard, dark, and unapproachable. But often, those mental assessments we make about people are wrong.

When it comes to approaching people, it is absolutely true that you cannot judge a book by its

177

cover. Often the people that I thought would turn me away are the very ones that say, "Yes! Please pray for me!" At other times, the people that look very friendly, open, and inviting are actually the ones that say, "No! Leave me alone. I don't want any part of it!"

Go ahead—walk up to somebody with a friendly smile on your face and say, "Excuse me, my name is _____. I pray for people and God heals them. Could I pray for you? Do you have any pain in your body?"

Sometimes they'll say, "I have no pain in my body."

You continue on and say, "Is there anything else in your life you would like me to pray for you about?"

Sometimes they'll say, "Well, I have family issues," or "I have job issues," or "I have financial issues." Whatever they bring up, pray about it. Take them as far as they'll let you take them.

I may tell them, "I don't believe it's chance that our paths have crossed and we are meeting each other today. I believe that God has arranged this moment. So may I pray for you?" If they say yes and allow me to pray for them, then I will usually say, "I am going to pray for you and you don't have to do anything but relax and receive."

I have found that if they pray with me, it often interferes because they may not be praying with the same understanding or level of faith. Also, as I am trying to pour into them and they are pouring out, this can sometimes hinder their receiving.

That was the case with a young man I met named Oliver. I met Oliver in a mall. When Oliver moved his neck or back, he experienced shooting pain at a level of about four of five. In Oliver's situation, I wanted to do something a little different.

Instead of praying for Oliver out loud, I handed him a card that I had delegated the authority to heal to. That's right—if Jesus can delegate to me, I can delegate to others. Even cards!

"That's interesting," Oliver said after a moment of holding the card. He twisted and turned in his seat. "I'm working harder to feel any pain."

Oliver didn't seem to fully grasp that he was being healed! But he was being healed, and he just needed to relax and receive it.

Just in case the part about delegating healing authority to an object sounds strange to you, I'll note this Scripture from Acts: "God did extraordinary miracles through Paul, so that even handkerchiefs and aprons that had touched him were taken to the sick, and their illnesses were cured and the evil spirits left them" (Acts 19:11-12 NIV). It might be strange, but it is 100% biblical!

Now, you don't necessarily have to do these things exactly the way I do them. The particular mechanisms I describe in this book are just what I have found works for me. When starting out, it's best to be open to different ways and methods and mechanisms God might want to use to heal people. In time you will learn what works for you, and you will have an approach all your own. It is important that you tailor your approach to match your own personality. If it is too canned or rehearsed, you will not come across as genuine.

READY, SET, ACTION!

People from all over the world have discovered God's healing power and salvation without ever leaving their home by watching videos of healings. If you would like to record your encounters, I have found a pretty successful method of getting people to permit me to film.

I don't walk up to them with a camera in their face. That is a big turn-off. I don't say, "Can I film this?" because they are not sure what you are going to do with it and they might be afraid that you would do something that would embarrass them.

Instead I say, "I teach people how to pray for folks. Would you mind if I record it?" Most of the time, they will allow me to record the encounter because when they see that I am doing something for the purpose of teaching others. This seems like a much more worthy cause than just putting something on YouTube so that your channel can get more views.

Almost all of my videos have been recorded on a GoPro camera because it is compact, non–intimidating, and it produces a high-quality image. As far as using a tripod, I don't. I have become pretty competent at holding it with my hand.

I have no zoom control. I have no viewfinder. I just point and shoot. That's all I'm doing because the less fussing with adjustments, the more comfortable the subject will be. I believe in making things as simple as possible.

As I hold the camera in one hand, I lay my other hand on the subject. If the subject is a woman, I'll ask permission to place my hand on them. Then, I place my hand near the place of pain or infirmity. If the pain is in a more sensitive location on her body, I'll have the woman put her hand on the infirmity and then I'll touch her hand with mine.

Prior to praying for the subject, I will ask them to assess their pain level by assigning it a number from one to 10. Then I will tell them to relax and receive my prayer. When they relax, they become more receptive to your prayers. If they are Christians, I will tell them, "Please don't pray, just let me pray." You don't want anything conflicting with your prayer.

Now, let's suppose the subject has a bad right knee, for example. I'll say, "I speak to this right knee. Knee, I command you to be made whole right now in Jesus' name! Muscles, tendons, ligaments, and nerves, be healed now!"

"Now" is the word that I say right before I silence my mind and think nothing. "Now" is like pulling the trigger, and the moment that follows is the silent watching to see when the bullet strikes the target. "Now" is a word that tells the infirmity not to simply go "someday" in the future. "Now" is a command that tells the infirmity *when* it must go.

If you were going to evict a deadbeat renter, you

wouldn't tell them to pack up and leave. Rather, you would give them a written notification that would specify a date they must be gone. You have authority. Use it to its fullest extent and be specific. I often address the pain separately after I command the healing.

PHYSICAL HEALING VERSUS PAIN HEALING

A physical healing and pain healing are two different healings.

Sometimes, it's not a pain issue, but a functional issue. Perhaps they have no pain, but they are blind, deaf, paralyzed, or simply can't raise their arm to a certain height or move their leg in a certain way. In those cases, you will need to have them test out the problem before you pray. After praying, ask them to test it again to see if they have improved. Or, in cases where a medical test is required, I ask them to follow up with me after their next medical appointment or test.

Take Angela's case, for example.

We hold healing services in our church on the first Sunday evening of each month. We get people coming in from all over the world for prayer. I have taught our congregation that any believer can pray and see miracles, and on this particular occasion, there were perhaps 20 people up front with me praying for the needs of the individuals who had come.

The next person standing in line came to me and told me her name was Angela. Angela was about 35 years old, and standing next to her was her daughter who was about 16. They both looked very healthy, so I asked what they needed prayer for.

Angela told me that she had been diagnosed with breast cancer and had tumors, one on her breast as well as one on her forearm. I prayed for the cancer to go and for her to be completely healed.

We looked at the tumor on her forearm and it had begun to flatten out. Neither Angela nor her daughter could believe it.

I then told Angela to go to her doctor and have him look for the tumors. A short time later Angela came to my office and told me that the doctor couldn't find any cancer in her body. In fact, her results were so confounding that he sent her in for more detailed and accurate tests. I told Angela that when it was all over, I wanted to hear about it and I also wanted medical documentation of the results.

Several weeks later Angela came back to my office with the documentation in her hands and the lump on her forearm flattened out completely.

The video of this testimony can be found on my YouTube page under the video titled: *Breast Cancer Tumor Vanishes in Jesus Name! – Tom Loud*

When it comes to pain, you first ask their level of pain. Then you say, "Excellent, we're going to take that down to a zero." That sounds pretty bold, but it is a step of faith. I have found that when I say it, the Lord backs up my faith-filled words with better results than if I don't say it.

For example, Derek. I met Derek in a parking

garage. Derek had severe neuropathy on his right side as a result of his diabetes. If you do not already know, diabetic neuropathy can be quite serious and debilitating —as it was in Derek's case. When I asked Derek his pain level, he said it was a twelve. Instead of praying for him myself, I had a guy I was training named Matt pray for him.

Matt prayed and then rested a moment. I asked Derek to check his pain. He looked dumbfounded, feeling around his leg. His reaction was one of the most sincere I've ever witnessed. He couldn't form a sentence —he just kept feeling his right leg, mouth agape.

I asked him how long he'd had the pain previously.

"Eight years."

After Derek realized that he had truly been healed, tears sprang to his eyes. He couldn't believe he'd finally been set free.

This isn't about a formulated prayer. This is about walking with your Father, knowing that He has authorized you to use His authority, and knowing that no matter how you say it or what you do, He will back you up.

Sometimes, I pray for them silently, and at other times, I say words. You're going to have to try different things and find out what works best for you. You are also going to need to be sensitive to the leading of the Holy Spirit, because sometimes, God will direct you to do things a certain way in a specific situation.

God will honor you because you are doing the Father's business. As you begin to step out of your comfort zone, in faith, expect that your Father will go with you. Believe that He is for you, and that He will back you up. And He will.

YOU CAN DO THIS!

Perhaps this proposition sounds a bit too outside of the box for you. Perhaps this is something you have never done and aren't even certain that you can do. Yes, those are thoughts that you may be having, but thoughts are just thoughts. They have no substance and are not necessarily true.

I want you to know this–the more that you step out and just do it, the bolder you will become. And what actually happens is that after you do it for a while, you begin to love it because that's what God made you for– His service.

I have a friend who was a paratrooper in the Army. Sometimes, people join the Army thinking that they are going to get to do one thing, but the Army has other ideas. You may sign up and think you're going to learn computers, but they decide they want you to be a paratrooper. You could protest and tell them that you have a fear of heights and they may say, "Well, that's too bad, because you will be jumping!"

Next thing you know, you're sitting in a classroom learning about gravity and what to do as soon as you leave that plane. This might be your worst nightmare, but your instructor is not interested in your personal problems. After the classroom comes the physical training. You are told to climb towers of various heights and then, connected to a zip-line, you're commanded, "Jump!" After a while, in spite of your pleading and reasoning, the day comes to jump out of a plane.

You say, "No! I can't do it!"

The instructor says, "Either you do it, or you're going to end up in federal prison!"

So you suit up and get in the plane, but you are scared to death. Then the moment comes when you are standing in a line of men about to jump. Before you know it, it's your turn.

The jumpmaster says to you, "Jump!"

You say, "I can't. I'm afraid!"

Do you know what happens next? They push you out. If you go up, you will go out.

Somehow, you survive. You say to yourself, "Thank God that is over. I will never do that again!"

The next thing you know, you're back in that plane again. For the first 10 jumps, they are quite happy to push you out. But somewhere along the line, you decide that you don't want their help, so you just jump.

After 20 times or so, you've resigned yourself to the fact that you are going to have to obey orders even if it kills you. But then comes jump number 50, and this time when the jumpmaster says jump, you don't bat an eyelid. You just jump. Suddenly, you realize that you're over it.

You're no longer afraid. Jumping is no longer a big deal. The more that you do something you are afraid of, the less afraid you will become. You may even find that after the fear is gone, you actually develop a pleasure in doing the thing you once dreaded.

So, ready or not, let's get started!

Plan to go. Set a date to go out alone or with a partner and keep that date. With prayer and intention, go out to a mall or to a park and politely walk up to whoever God places in your path. You may be saying, "But what if I fail?"

Well, I have two things to say about that. The first is, "You can't fail because stepping out and doing kingdom business is obeying God's Word and doing God's work. Obedience is never counted as a failure." Failure would be if you failed to go.

The second is, "What if you are successful?" Well, that would be life-changing for both you and the person you're praying for. We initiate the contact. That is our part and then the Lord does the miracle. That is His part. Just do your part and leave the rest to Jesus!

Finally, I would never leave a baby out in the woods at the mercy of the wolves. So I always give contact information to the people I am ministering to. When you're ministering, give them a card from your church or your personal number so they can be supported, so they can know that there is always someone there for them to reach out to when they need help or direction.

GO!

Jesus said to the twelve, "Come." That was His first command to them. But after He trained them, and just before He was caught up into Heaven to sit at the right hand of God, He gave them another command: "Go!"

> He said to them, "Go into all the world and preach the gospel to all creation. Whoever believes and is baptized will be saved, but whoever does not believe will be condemned. And these signs will accompany those who believe: In my name they will drive out demons; they will speak in new tongues; they will pick up snakes with their hands; and when they drink deadly poison, it will not hurt them at all; they will place their hands on sick people, and they will get well."

> After the Lord Jesus had spoken to them, he was taken up into heaven and he sat at the right hand of God. Then the disciples went out and preached everywhere, and the Lord worked with them and confirmed his word by the signs that accompanied it.

> — MARK 16:15-20 NIV

When you opened this book, you already had all the keys you needed to operate in the supernatural.

You have the key of identity as a child of God. You have the key of the authority of Christ through his death and resurrection. You have the key of the Spirit mind through God's Holy Spirit. You have the key to overcoming the carnal mind by commanding it into silence. Finally, you have the key of calling, knowing that Jesus has not only asked you to go preach His kingdom, but He has commanded it.

You have answered the "come" by choosing to follow Christ.

All that's left now is for you to "go!"

ACKNOWLEDGMENTS

I would like to give special thanks to my friend Pete Cabrera Jr. for all of his insight, inspiration, and encouragement and also to Michael Chen, who was instrumental in making this book possible.

I would also like to thank all of my friends and family at Shoreline Full Gospel Fellowship and Royal Family International University. Thank you all and may God bless you richly!

PUBLISHER'S NOTE: AN INVITATION TO PARADISE

CALLED WRITERS
CHRISTIAN PUBLISHING

All of us wonder why there is pain in the world. We struggle with questions like, "Why would a good God allow so much suffering?" When we ask that question, what we're effectively saying is, "Why doesn't God do something?" We struggle to understand why He doesn't step in and put an end to human suffering once and for all.

The reality is, He is going to do that very thing. One day, He will physically step back into the scene. He is going to put His foot on the Mount of Olives in Jerusalem, and begin the process of restoring earth to its former glory and perfection. The Bible describes the future earth this way:

Then I saw "a new heaven and a new earth," for the first heaven and the first earth had passed away, and there was no longer any sea. I saw the Holy City, the new Jerusalem, coming down out of heaven from God, prepared as a bride beautifully dressed for her husband. And I heard a loud voice from the throne saying, "Look! God's dwelling place is now among the people, and he will dwell with them. They will be his people, and God himself will be with them and be their God. 'He will wipe every tear from their eyes. There will be no more death' or mourning or crying or pain, for the old order of things has passed away."

He who was seated on the throne said, "I am making everything new!"

— REVELATION 21:1-5 NIV

No more tears. No more pain.

The world that we all long for is coming.

It's on the way.

The big question is: Will you be part of that new world?

In order to be part of that new world, we must receive Jesus Christ as Lord and Savior. There will be pleasures beyond anything we can imagine in that new world. In fact, one of the first things we will experience there is a huge party called, "The Wedding Feast of the Lamb." There will be wine, music, dancing, celebration, and immense joy.

But there will not be any rebellion against God.

The only people who will be in God's new world

will be the ones who chose to love Him and give their lives to Him. Just like Jesus asked His disciples, "Who do you say that I am?" we must all answer that same question.

WHO IS JESUS?

God the Father sent His One and Only Son, Jesus Christ, to this imperfect world to redeem us and restore us into a free and open relationship with Himself. Because humankind had sinned, our relationship with God was broken. Severed. And we were under the penalty of sin, which is punishment and death.

Instead of leaving us to suffer those penalties, Jesus decided to take our place. He took our punishment for us by dying a gruesome death on the cross. Jesus was then buried, and on the third day, He was resurrected into eternal life. He defeated death and the grave, and that means we can now freely receive forgiveness for all of our sins.

GOD'S OFFER TO EVERYONE

Eternal life with God in His perfect world is offered to all of us.

If we choose to reject this offer, that means we are choosing sin over God. We are choosing to stay in rebellion toward Him. This will be the result for those who choose to stay in rebellion toward God:

"But the cowardly, the unbelieving, the vile, the murderers, the sexually immoral, those who practice magic arts, the idolaters and all liars— they will be consigned to the fiery lake of burning sulfur. This is the second death."

— REVELATION 21:8 NIV

When presented with options in life, we all want to make the best decision. We weigh all of our important decisions, and we choose carefully.

You can make the right choice today. At this very moment, you are being given the option to end your rebellion toward God, turn away from sin, and choose to receive His forgiveness. You can choose right now to receive Christ as Savior.

A PRAYER FOR SALVATION

If you want to receive Christ as Savior, here is a prayer you can pray right now:

God, I want to live in Heaven with You forever. I do not want to live in sin and rebellion. No human being is perfect, including me. I have done things that You say are wrong. Please forgive me of all my sins, and please give me a new life with You. I now receive Jesus Christ as my Lord and Savior.

Thank you, God, for saving me!

This section of the book is a note from the publisher to share the Gospel of Jesus Christ and invite you, the reader, into a relationship with Him. The reason for this invitation is simple: We want every human being alive to go to Heaven. If you made a decision to receive Christ as Savior today, please reach out to us at CalledWriters.com and let us know.

We want to celebrate with you, and also help you with next steps. God bless you!

RECENT RELEASES FROM CALLED WRITERS

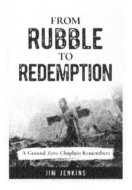

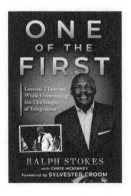

**SECURING OUR IDENTITY
AS CHRISTIANS**

BISHOP ERIC A. LAMBERT, JR.
with CHRIS MCKINNEY

DON'T DO ANYTHING STUPID

**A WHITE MAN'S GUIDE
TO RACIAL HARMONY**

JOHN COVINGTON

THE
Jericho
FAST

How to Break through Walls
with Prayer and Fasting

RHODA FAYE DIEHL

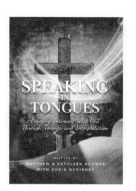

ABOUT THE AUTHOR

Tom Loud is the Senior Pastor of Shoreline Full Gospel Fellowship, located in the greater Seattle area. He has been in ministry for more than 40 years. Since 2014, Tom has taught and led marketplace ministry around the world, crossing many denominational lines. After being given a revelation by the Holy Spirit in 2014, Tom has seen thousands of healing miracles and has taught many others around the world how to see God heal people supernaturally through their prayers and outreach efforts.

Tom's YouTube channel has gotten millions of views by demonstrating God's miraculous power to save, heal, and deliver people. There is plenty of teaching and training freely available on his YouTube channel. Tom also personally teaches and trains anyone who has a desire to participate in this type of outreach, and he does so free of charge.

For free teaching and training sessions in the Seattle area, or to have Tom speak at your church, please contact: office@shorelinefullgospel.org

Tom can also be reached personally at PastorTomLoud@gmail.com

Made in United States
North Haven, CT
18 July 2022

21543379R00125